What Makes a Woman Feel Loved?

EMILIE BARNES

HARVEST HOUSE PUBLISHERS

EUGENE, OREGON

Cover by Dugan Design Group, Bloomington, Minnesota

Cover photo © Laurence Mouton / PhotoAlto / Getty Images

WHAT MAKES A WOMAN FEEL LOVED
Copyright © 2007 by Emilie Barnes
Published by Harvest House Publishers
Eugene, Oregon 97402
www.harvesthousepublishers.com

Library of Congress Cataloging-in-Publication Data
   Barnes, Emilie.
   What makes a woman feel loved / Emilie Barnes.
      p. cm.
   ISBN-13: 978-0-7369-2133-6 (pbk.)
   ISBN-10: 0-7369-2133-8 (pbk.)
   1. Sex differences—Religious aspects—Christianity. 2. Marriage—Religious aspects—Christianity. I. Title.
   BT708.B36 2007
   248.8'425—dc22
                                                                            2007002504

Printed in the United States of America

07 08 09 10 11 12 13 14 15 / VP-SK / 12 11 10 9 8 7 6 5 4 3 2 1

To all the men I know who have shown love to their wives. Through God's grace and His miracles, you have found the keys that unlock the mysteries of marriage. You have been willing to be submissive to God and the principles taught in the Bible.

You have been men who started out to love your spouses. In return, you found you were the real winners in life. The more you love your mate, the more love you will receive from her.

Thanks for sharing your lives with me. You are marvelous examples of what God can do in a man's life when he loves his wife.

Contents

Introduction

I have written more than 60 books. That's thousands of pages to help women make their lives more productive and become women with hearts dedicated to God.

After doing hundreds of seminars on home and marriage issues and talking to thousands of women, I have some words of wisdom that will assist you in knowing what makes women tick and what makes them ticked.

I always tell my audiences that men are weird and women are strange. God designed us that way so we can't completely figure out the other sex. This is part of the mystery that attracts us to each other. In fact, a humorist once told of a conversation God had with Adam, His first creation:

> God saw that Adam enjoyed the Garden of Eden and all of its beauty, but he was looking sad and knew that something was missing from his life. God approached Adam and said, "Adam, you have been so faithful here in the Garden, I would like to grant you one wish." Adam excitedly knew his wish and said, "God, I would like you to build me a bridge that stretches from Southern California to Hawaii."
>
> God pondered the wish for a moment, and then told Adam that it was impossible to build such a bridge— an engineering impossibility. However, since He was not

able to grant that wish, He told Adam that he could have another wish.

Without hesitation, Adam requested from God, "God, when you give me a wife, would it also be possible to give me a handbook on how to understand women?"

God frowned a little bit, and then He uttered these words, "Do you want a two-lane or four-lane bridge to Hawaii?"

That's a funny story and we laugh, but unfortunately it is often true. We women can be hard to figure out. We are all uniquely created and very different from men. My Bob tells me when he thinks he has me figured out, I change.

In this book I'll help you unlock the secrets of how to thoroughly love your wife. At the end of each chapter I have included a section called *Pillow Talk*. These are questions you can ask your wife when you go to bed at night. I guarantee that these questions will lead to remarkable adventures in communication. They will provide valuable experiences to loving and knowing your wife better. You can also discuss these questions and your answers from a male perspective.

I've also included a section called *Love Gestures*[1] that shares comments wives have said regarding what their husbands do right—the things that women love to hear and have done for them.

I know that if you read these pages you will have greater tools to understand your wife and be able to love her better. All women want to be loved—and it helps to know our language so we can better understand your message of love!

Emilie

1

Experiencing Love

Love is patient, love is kind...
[Love] always protects,
always trusts, always hopes,
always perseveres.

1 CORINTIHIANS 13:4,7

Helen Keller wrote this delightful explanation of love:

> I remember the morning that I first asked the meaning of the word "love." This was before I knew many words. I had found a few early violets in the garden and brought them to my teacher. She tried to kiss me, but at that time I did not like to have anyone kiss me except my mother. Miss Sullivan put her arm gently around me and spelled into my hand, "I love Helen."
>
> "What is love?" I asked.
>
> She drew me closer to her and said, "It is here," pointing to my heart....
>
> Her words puzzled me very much because I did not then understand anything unless I touched it. I smelled the violets in her hand and asked, half in words, half in signs, a question which meant "Is love the sweetness of flowers?"
>
> "No," said my teacher.
>
> Again I thought. The warm sun was shining on us.

"Is this not love?" I asked, pointing in the direction from which the heat came.

A day or two afterward...the sun had been under a cloud all day, and there had been brief showers, but suddenly the sun broke forth in all its southern splendor. Again I asked my teacher, "Is this not love?"

"Love is something like the clouds that were in the sky before the sun came out," she replied. Then in simpler words than these, which at that time I could not have understood, she explained: "You cannot touch the clouds, you know, but you feel the rain and know how glad the flowers and the thirsty earth are to have it after a hot day. You cannot touch love either; but you feel the sweetness that it pours into everything. Without love you would not be happy or want to play."

The beautiful truth burst upon my mind—I felt that these were invisible lines stretched between my spirit and the spirit of others.

Throughout Scripture we read of love, love, love. Can we smell it? Can we feel it? Can we taste it? Can we hear it? Men, when you love your wives, all of their senses will light up. There's nothing more beautiful and exciting than a wife who feels loved.

Express Your Love

Give your wife the night off. You fix dinner and clean up afterward. Get your kids to help.

Knowing the Foundations for Love

Before you can fully love your wife, you must first realize from a biblical point of view why you are to love—and what means there are to get to that result. No Christian growth is possible without obedience to the Scriptures.

The "natural man" must have a change of heart before he can make changes toward godly outward obedience. In 2 Chronicles 34:33 we read, "Throughout [Josiah's] lifetime they did not turn from following the LORD God of their fathers," and in Joshua 24:15, Joshua asserts, "As for me and my house, we will the serve the LORD." These two verses tell us that there must be a commitment by each of us to choose to worship God before we can step out in action and truly love one another.

> But now faith, hope, love, abide these three;
> but the greatest of these is love.
>
> 1 CORINTHIANS 13:13

Love given to another person must first be given to God. John 14:15 tells us Jesus said, "If you love Me, you will keep My commandments." When He was asked, "Which is the great commandment in the Law?" Jesus answered, "You shall love the Lord your God with all your heart, and with all your soul, and with all your mind." Then He said, "The second is like it, 'You shall love your neighbor as yourself'" (Matthew 22:36-39).

It is obvious that God gives us a guideline that we are to love Him first before we are able to truly love anyone else. Men, you are to love God first, and then you can think about loving your wives. A godly woman yearns for a man who will worship God. She understands that if you can love God and put Him first in your life, you are then able to truly love her sacrificially.

A successful life is lived by one who has the right priorities in his life—being obedient to God's Word—and then putting into action what he knows to be true. Love is really acting out in all relationships what you know to be true about the love of God. If you have not made the decision to love and serve God in your life, then seek out a friend or pastor who can lead you through that process. Your understanding of love will increase dramatically!

Love is expressed when you stop living life your way and turn to living life God's way. When your marriage is based on God's principles, then your loving leadership in the family builds trust and security for your wife and your children.

Christian growth is a long, often difficult process. However, if you as the husband will be committed to the headship of Jesus in your family and to the authority of Scripture (2 Timothy 3:16), these priorities will give you the inspiration and courage you need to live responsibly. When you live like this, your wife and children will have a true sense of being loved.

> There is no fear in love; but perfect love casts out fear.
>
> 1 John 4:18

All of us spend a good part of our lives earnestly searching for the most rewarding feeling of all—love. As tiny babes, we look to those around us to give us love. Later on in life, we read books and magazines, attend workshops and seminars, and have long conversations with others attempting to improve our understanding of love.

Despite our best efforts, we still have a hard time defining love. So what is this sought-after feeling? According to Scripture, it's much more than a fleeting emotion. Instead, *love is a decision* that we consciously make each day, and its presence is revealed in how we treat our spouses and others. When we love them, we choose to do what's best for them. The ultimate example of this kind of love is found in the primary love God has for us: "For God so loved the world, that He gave His only begotten Son, that whoever believes in Him shall not perish, but have eternal life" (John 3:16).

Now that's love! In spite of our not always choosing to do things His way, God gave us His only Son so that we might be forgiven and delight in His everlasting caring. When we are able to capture even a glimpse of the magnitude of God's love, we gain an immense understanding of what love is all about. And we gradually discover that He has placed in us a capacity to love others far beyond what we could ever imagine. Through this we begin to love God, love ourselves, and love others. In fact, this becomes our main mission of life. This kind of love—*agape* love, the highest expression of love—can conquer all. It comes directly from heaven. When it enters our hearts, we are truly blessed with its rewards.

Pillow Talk

- How much importance do you place on academic education?
- If you could talk to God face-to-face and ask one question, what would it be?
- Do you have a hero? Who is it and why?
- What is your happiest memory?
- What would be your ideal vacation?

Love Gestures

- I love a man who can be tough and tender.
- I love a man who values my opinions.
- I love a man who gives me financial security.
- I love a man who washes my car.
- I love a man who cuts my hair and gives me a pedicure.
- I love a man who will really listen to me.

Making a Great Marriage

A happy marriage is the union
of two good forgivers.

ROBERT QUILLEN

Since Bob and I now have gray hair and have been together so long, young couples are always asking us, "What makes a great marriage?" At this stage in life I can be very direct in my response: "God's Word has been the foundation for a great marriage for Bob and me. We have often said it in the form of an equation: God's prescription + our committed efforts = marital fullness."

As we have worked to apply God's teachings to our marriage, we have discovered five principles for growing a great marriage. We use the following "GREAT" acrostic to relate these principles to others:

G—Giving

R—Relating

E—Edifying

A—Allowing your mate to be God's person

T—Touching

Giving

God's nature is to give, and He is continually giving His free gifts to us. His plan for us is to be continual givers also. In marriage that means we must give to one another our time, our talents, our hearts, ourselves, our love, our finances, our gifts, our thoughts, our trust, and our fears.

> Getters generally don't get happiness; givers get it. You simply give to others a bit of yourself— a thoughtful act, a helpful idea, a word of appreciation, a lift over a rough spot, a sense of under- standing, a timely suggestion. You take something out of your mind, garnished in kindness out of your heart, and put it into the other fellow's mind and heart.
>
> CHARLES H. BURR

When Bob and I stopped thinking about ourselves and started giving to each other, our relationship improved. Some of the little gifts we have given each other that have received positive responses are notes sent through the mail, a card of love tucked in a purse or lunch sack, words of encouragement, a bouquet of flowers, a new book to discuss, time in the evening for conversation, mini-vacations together, and dinner out at least twice a month.

We also found that when we started giving to each other, it became easier for us to give to others. The circle of giving soon spread to people we didn't even know.

Relating

We live in a day when everyone wants to relate. The dictionary defines relating as "one person connecting with another in thought and meaning." If any two people must connect in thought and meaning, it is husband and wife! Relating is a primary avenue to oneness in marriage. This can only happen when partners spend much time together talking, listening, and learning what makes each other tick and ticked. This is very difficult for people who don't express themselves well. I was very hesitant to speak during Bob's and my early courtship because I feared I would say the wrong thing and blow our relationship. With Bob's encouragement, I overcame my shyness. Now I have no trouble expressing myself. I give my Bob much of the credit for improving my ability to relate not only with him, but with others.

A passage of Scripture we often use when teaching couples how to relate is Proverbs 24:3-4: "By wisdom a house is built, and by understanding it is established; and by knowledge the rooms are filled with all precious and pleasant riches." There are three key words that stand out in these two verses:

- wisdom
- understanding
- knowledge

We gain these three qualities by studying the Scriptures, reading relevant books, and attending workshops and seminars. We can't learn these three strengths by doing nothing. We have to be active in acquiring them.

In marriage we are to study our mates thoroughly in order to gain wisdom, understanding, and knowledge about them. How do we study them? By relating to them through open, genuine conversation.

> The only basis for real fellowship with God and man is to live out in the open with both.
> ROY HESSION

One man I heard about lost $250,000 through the stock market. How would you react if you watched a quarter of a million dollars disappear before your very eyes? Would you jump off a bridge or get drunk? Fortunately, this man had learned that his home was a "trauma center." He phoned his wife and calmly told her what had happened. Then he asked her for a date that evening. They went out to dinner and discussed the day's happening together, just like they had done many times before over far less shattering events. Thank the Lord this couple had learned to relate!

Relating doesn't happen automatically. Growing in communication takes a lot of hard, well-planned work. Marital wisdom, understanding, and knowledge come through many patient hours of relating. But there is a reward for our labors. The "precious and pleasant riches" we gain from our efforts are positive attitudes, good relationships, pleasant memories, mutual respect, and depth in character.

Edifying

One way a wife feels loved is when her husband and children lift her up with praise. Women (actually everyone!) just love to hear words that build them up. Words and phrases such as...

- Mom, this was really a good breakfast.
- Thanks for supporting me at school.
- You are really a great mom and wife.
- You make me feel like a king when I come home.
- I really appreciate how you make our house a home.

Communication is a major channel by which we edify one another. If our goal is to lift someone up, we make a choice to be positive in our words and action while around her. We realize that positive words build up and heal, while negative words destroy and tear down.

One way to check our attitude is to constantly ask, "Is this edifying?" If not, shape up and go positive. Each person would do well to keep that question in the forefront of his mind to make sure the conversation stays encouraging.

> It takes so little to make us sad,
> Just a slighting word or doubting sneer,
> Just a scornful smile on some lips held dear;
> And our footsteps lag, though the goal seemed near,
> And we lose our courage and hope we had—
> So little it takes to make us sad.
>
> It takes so little to make us glad,
> Just a cheering clasp of a friendly hand,
> Just a word from one who can understand;
> And we finish the task we long had planned,
> And we lose the doubt and the fear we had—
> So little it takes to make us glad.
>
> IDA GOLDSMITH MORRIS

Allowing Your Mate to Be God's Person

One of the hardest lessons about trusting God in our marriages is allowing Him to be the change agent in our mates. Far too often we think we are ordained by God to change them. One way to deal with the urge to change our mates is to concentrate on the positives and let God deal with the negatives. You might use a chart like the one on the next page to help you and your mate identify areas that you would like to improve in your lives with the help of the Holy Spirit. Remember, although you can mention areas you'd like your mate to think about, the change is up to her and God. Don't nag. And you also must be open to her suggested changes.

Like you and your wife, Bob and I have always wanted the best for each other. One of our goals has been to avoid competition between us. We are to complement each other. If one of us gets lifted up in some fashion, the other says, "Thank You, God, for blessing Bob/Emilie."

When Bob was in education, I was always known as Bob's wife. But for the last several years, since God has blessed my writing and speaking ministry, Bob has been known as my husband. This reversal initially was a threat to him, even though he was excited for me. Bob had always been the main provider, and he loved the spotlight. Suddenly he was playing second fiddle behind me. He had to ask himself if he wanted to glorify himself or did he want to bring glory to God through my ministry. Every time the question was asked, the same answer came back—glorify God. It took some time for Bob to realize that he felt comfortable with this change in our lives. He can honestly say now that as long as Jesus is lifted up in *our* ministry, he will serve in whatever capacity Jesus wants to use him in.

It's so easy to get caught up in the world's mind-set of being in competition with everyone—including your mate. Satan would love to divide your strengths, talents, and gifts by seeing you work against each other. He will prey on your insecurities to drive a wedge between you and your spouse, fracturing your unity.

Category of Expectation	Strengths	Desired Changes	Action for Change
1. Personal habits	very neat picks up clothes hangs towels puts away shoes	to take a shower each day to shampoo hair regularly to use underarm deodorant	to talk to her about these areas to buy her her own shampoo and deodorant let God work in this area
2. Children			
3. Finances			
4. Sex			
5. Spiritual			
6. Social			
7. Aspirations			
8. Time			
9.			
10.			

Become encouragers to one another. Be excited about your mate's successes. Be there to comfort your partner when the contract isn't signed, the deal falls through, sickness slows her down, the license isn't renewed, and so forth. If you learn to submit to each other by the power of the Holy Spirit, you can allow each other to be God's worker.

Touching

Can you remember when a parent, teacher, or coach wrapped his or her arm around you or patted you gently to indicate that everything was going to be okay? A loving touch has healing power and communicates that we are accepted. If children live with touching parents, they too will learn to touch people in healthy ways and will be touchers themselves in adult life. We say around our home that everybody needs at least one hug a day to stay healthy.

Express Your Love

Give your wife a shoulder rub after her evening bath or shower. Tell her before you start that you don't want one in return. Let her truly relax and enjoy the experience.

Touching is also an important element in establishing a good marriage. Bob and I have found nonsexual touching to be an excellent way to transmit helpful encouragement to each other. Unfortunately, when choosing a mate we seldom consider if the prospective partner is a toucher. Some of us come from very affectionate families, some do not. It's hard for nontouchers to become touchers, but with prayer and patience, even the most reserved nontoucher can become a loving toucher.

Men: Most women like a hug, an arm around the shoulders, holding hands in a movie, a gentle neck rub. She perceives your touch as saying, "I love you." And touching doesn't always have to lead to the bedroom, which is many times the man's goal. Touching from your wife doesn't necessarily mean you will wind up there, either. However, don't always rule out that objective.

Affectionate touching between Mom and Dad also signals to the children that their parents love each other. Children are comforted by the security of knowing their parents are lovingly committed to each other.

These five elements of a great marriage don't just happen. They must be cultivated like a good crop of corn. The mere presence of these elements doesn't guarantee the success of a marriage, but having them certainly holds the potential to enrich an already strong marriage or energize a slumping one.

The following lines are worth reading, rereading, and pondering. They communicate volumes about great marriages:

- All marriages aren't happy; living together is tough.
- A good marriage is not a gift; it's an achievement by God's grace.
- Marriage is not for children; it takes guts and maturity.
- Marriage separates the men from the boys and the women from the girls.
- Marriage is tested daily by the ability to compromise.
- The survival of marriage can depend on being smart enough to know what's worth fighting about, making a issue of, or even mentioning.
- Marriage is giving and, more importantly, forgiving.
- With all its ups and downs, marriage is still God's best object lesson of Jesus and the church.

> Remember, the choices you make today will determine the kind of marriage you will have in the years to come, so choose wisely. Choose love for a lifetime.
>
> RICHARD EXLEY

- Through submission to one another we can witness to the world that marriage does work and is still alive.
- Marriage is worth dying for. If we give it proper honor, we will be honored by our children, our families, our neighbors, our friends, and—best of all—our Lord.

Pillow Talk

- What person gave you the most spiritual guidance in your life?
- If you could start over at a specific time in your life, when would that be?
- If you only had one day left to live, how would you spend it?
- Describe the most memorable or special date you ever had.
- Share an exciting day trip you would enjoy going on.

Love Gestures

- I love a man who will massage my feet.
- I love a man who will go to chick flicks with me.
- I love a man who likes to look at me more than seeing himself in the mirror.
- I love a man who makes sure my automobile tires are in good condition.

3

Knowing What Love
Is All About

*I feel that God would sooner we
did wrong in loving than never
love for fear we should do wrong.*

FATHER ANDREW

Love is the most important element and the foundation of the relationship you have with your life mate. But the word *love* is used so loosely in the English language today. We love our pets, but that's different than loving our mates. We can love a piece of music, our child, or the cool breeze of a spring morning. There's even the term "love" in tennis. We are capable of loving a close friend, our jobs, and our favorite meals. Love also represents very different emotions. What sets apart the emotion we have for a wife or a special woman? Falling in love is surely different than these other loves.

Learning more about this word *love* will help us better understand how these relationships often start out like any other emotion, but then progress to the point where both people desire a lifetime commitment together.

Love is more than a feeling, and we all know from past experiences that feeling "in love" can be misleading and is often very fickle. Today the feeling is here, and tomorrow it's gone. Individuals who make decisions based on their feelings are usually unstable in other areas of their lives.

Scripture gives a very clear definition of what biblical love is about. First Corinthians 13:4-7 is probably the most-used Scripture at wedding ceremonies (in both religious and nonreligious weddings):

> Love is patient, love is kind. It does not envy, it does not boast, it is not proud. It is not rude, it is not self-seeking, it is not easily angered, it keeps no record of wrongs. Love does not delight in evil but rejoices with the truth. It always protects, always trusts, always hopes, always perseveres (NIV).

Scripture describes three types of love. *"Eros,"* or erotic love, is driven by our physical attraction to another individual. We feel sexual desire toward that person. This type of love can arrive quickly and has a very strong appeal. Young love is usually this type. As men (because you are more visual than women), you need to distinguish this as a "red flag" in a relationship. Eros certainly has its place in a marriage relationship, and a well-rounded, intimate relationship will certainly have this type of love evident. But eros love, if not discriminately used, can end up controlling your life. This is an emotion that needs to be controlled *by* you. Don't be carried away by your senses during your early courtship. Eros love occurs and is important in females, but it usually develops at a slower pace than with males.

Love is a fruit in season at all times, and within reach of every hand. Anyone may gather it, and no limit is set. Everyone can reach this love through meditation, spirit of prayer, and sacrifice, by an intense inner life.

MOTHER TERESA

The second type of love mentioned in Scripture is *"philo,"* and it's often referred to as "brotherly love." This kind of love is one you share with a close friend. It comes about after spending a great deal of time with someone. That's why many marriage counselors recommend that courtship before marriage should last a minimum of one year. The more we know about an individual, the more likely we will become a "philo friend." Married love is healthiest when it comes out of a friendship relationship. That's one of the purposes of dating. We get a chance to truly know the one we are going out with. This love is extremely important in finding your life mate. Philo love can be extended to your next door neighbor, a teammate in sports, a fellow worker, someone leading a small group of which you are a member.

How are we led to have this type of love? Not like eros, which is based on physical attraction. Philo is developed as a person's character traits and interests become known by you, and you realize that those traits are ones you value.

Your wife should be your favorite friend of the opposite sex. However, you can and should have other philo friends of your gender. Men tend to be loners. I encourage you to have several other friends. Be careful when dealing with ladies who want to be friends when you are married, though. We all need to have acquaintances, but we also must guard our hearts when it comes to having friends of the opposite sex.

Express Your Love

Give your wife a big hug and tell her thank you for all she does to make home so warm and fun.

We develop philo love when we spend time together—by going on picnics, hiking, sharing sport activities, going to the theater, watching movies, sharing a bag of popcorn. Our philo friends bring out the best in us. We love to be around them. They help civilize and inspire us.

Men and women are different in how they progress from the first meeting to sexual fulfillment. Males tend to go from eros love to philo love, but females often develop philo first and then go to eros love. Your wife or girlfriend might make a statement such as,

"He grew on me!" What she is saying is that she developed eros love *after* getting to know you as a friend. Even after marriage, never forget this need of the woman in your life. She wants you to be her number one friend of the opposite sex.

Philo love can be turned off by the words we use. Words that convey anger, arrogance, self-pity, selfishness, resentment, and mistrust are negatives in your relationship. Guard your philo love with words that encourage, inspire, compliment, and show respect and appreciation.

"Agape" is the most common word for love in the New Testament. This love actively seeks to do the right thing for and meet the needs of the loved person. In this case, your wife. Agape sacrifices personal feelings and needs to meet the needs of your spouse. In agape we willingly give up our rights, our desires, and our demands to fulfill our partners'. We may come home from work too tired to be kind or romantic to our spouses who need our loving attention. But agape love moves beyond what we feel like doing. It patiently seeks to discover and meet the needs of the other, no matter what the personal cost may be. So we rise above ourselves and meet the needs of our spouses.

All facets of love must reside within the boundaries of agape love. Our goal as Christians is to allow agape love to penetrate and rule the other two dimensions of love in our lives. In order to allow agape its rightful place, we must first know Jesus Christ as our personal Savior and be submissive to His leadership. If you haven't made this basic commitment, you cannot move beyond eros and philo love. Many marriages can survive on these two dimensions of love alone, but it is God's will for Christians to allow agape love to dominate all of their relationships, bringing more depth and love to marriage. Agape love is the concrete in the foundation of a relationship that is ready to commit for life.

You can also have agape love for people to whom you are not married. Your children, your parents, your fellow Christians can all experience an agape love with you.

All three types of love should be experienced with that one person you wish to marry or are married to.

The more you know about love, the better you'll be able to love your wife.

Pillow Talk

- Describe your earliest memory.
- Can you think of an invention that would make this world better?
- What are your deepest fears?
- What is your favorite holiday tradition?
- Is it ever okay to keep secrets from your spouse?

Love Gestures

- I love a man who is strong yet sensitive.
- I love a man who calls me by a pet name.
- I love a man who puts his arm around my shoulders and says I love you.
- I love a man who has good hygiene.

4

Beyond the Wedding

If any of you lacks wisdom,
he should ask God, who gives
generously to all without finding
fault, and it will be given to him.

JAMES 1:5 NIV

Somewhere between the thrill of the engagement, the hectic preparation for the wedding, and the joy of the big day—and often despite excellent premarital counseling—the message gets lost, overlooked, or silenced. That message? Marriage takes effort and commitment.

Genesis 2:24 states, "A man shall leave his father and his mother, and be joined to his wife; and they shall become one flesh." Those 21 words of this verse tell it all. They sum up the complete teaching on marriage in the Scripture. As Bob and I studied this passage, we saw that God was calling us to:

- Departure
- Permanence
- Oneness

Departure

Besides physically leaving their parents' homes, both the husband and wife are to become emotionally and financially independent as well. The marriage relationship—and the new family that has been created—is to be the primary source of emotional health, financial provision, security, and protection for the couple.

The bonds of love for one's parents are everlasting, but these connections are to change. The new couple will not make an absolute break from their parents, but they must realize that they are now a family, and they need to make their own decisions. The new husband and wife must have greater loyalty to each other than to their parents. An early Jewish custom was that the husband was to do nothing the first year of marriage except get to know his wife. That's how important total commitment was to the Jewish family. This meant the husband would not go to war, play in a baseball league, teach Sabbath school, or go on a fishing trip with the boys. Likewise the new bride was to learn about her new husband. No distractions along the way.

Physically moving from the parents' home is just one kind of necessary departure for a healthy marriage. Husbands and wives also need to depart emotionally. Too many married adults have never consciously stepped away from their parents' emotional control. The process of stepping away emotionally will be gradual, and that process is harder when strong, controlling parents are involved. In that case, the departing young adult may feel guilty about leaving, but such emotional separation is necessary and healthy. It doesn't mean that we no longer care about our parents; it simply means that we are not under parental control. Adults must continue to honor their parents (see Matthew 15:3-9 and 1 Timothy 5:4-8). The new couple must continually be ready to care for them and to assume responsibility *for* them rather than responsibility *to* them.

Financial independence is another important aspect of leaving home. Leaving financially means we are free to accept financial assistance from our parents, but we no longer depend on them for the funds we need. Again, many adults have not tried to achieve financial independence because they are counting on dad and mom's money to be there for them.

Achieving independence from one's parents can be a long or short, easy or difficult process. One way to make the separation easier on young people as well as their parents is to follow the example of our Jewish brothers and sisters. In the Jewish wedding ceremonies Bob and I have attended, parents of both the bride and groom recite vows releasing their children from their authority. Formally releasing one's children could serve to eliminate a lot of uncertainty, guilt, and unhealthy dependence as a new couple works to get established. Again, departure doesn't mean that parents and their married children will never see each other. It does mean a new phase of relationship in which parents regard their children as independent adults capable of managing their own homes, their own emotional lives, and their own financial situations.

You, as a husband, cannot freely give to your wife until you know in your heart that you are more important to her than any other person in her life. Likewise, your wife needs to know that she is the most important person in your life before she can be fully committed to you. We show our spouse that he or she holds that number one spot when, at every level, we leave our parents' house.

Permanence

According to Genesis 2:24, leaving one's father and mother is just the first step toward a strong and godly marriage. Next the verse states a man shall "be joined to his wife." The Hebrew word translated "joined" means "to cling" or "to be glued to" and clearly expresses God's intention that a husband and wife be bonded to one another permanently. Marriage is not an experiment or a trial run. Marriage is a once-and-for-all union. "Join" suggests determined action; there is nothing passive about this word.

In light of the fact that marriage should be permanent, God gives these instructions to a newly married couple: "When a man takes a new wife, he shall not go out with the army nor be charged with any duty; he shall be free at home one year and shall give happiness to his wife whom he has taken" (Deuteronomy 24:5). This period of time gave the couple the opportunity to get to know one another and build a foundation for a marriage that would last.

Few newlyweds today have the resources that would allow them to quit their jobs and spend every moment of their first year alone together. But there are some practical steps all married couples can take or apply to reinforce the glue of permanence in their marriage.

Leave your parents' homes and set up a home of your own. If at all possible, do not live in the same house with either of your parents—even if it is more economical to do so.

Spend as much time together as possible. Your marriage is to take priority over nights out with the boys. After all, we can't build relationships with our spouses that will last if we don't spend time together, especially when we're first married. Our spouses are more important than our friends, and our actions need to reflect that fact, even if old friends don't understand.

Reserve the bedroom for sleeping and loving. Do this by keeping the television out of your bedroom. Many husbands go to bed and watch the end of a movie, the late news, or the last play of a ball game. When this happens, the television robs many couples of the happiness they should be providing each other in the bedroom.

Permanence isn't valued in our culture today, but it's valued by our God, the one who established marriage for us. Furthermore, permanence doesn't happen automatically. It takes work—but the rewards make the work well worth the effort.

Oneness

After calling husbands and wives to leave their fathers and mothers and be joined to one another, God says that the two "shall become one flesh" (Genesis 2:24). In God's sight, we become one at the altar when we say our vows to one another before Him, but, practically speaking, oneness between a husband and wife is a *process* that happens over a period of time—over their lifetime together.

Becoming one can be a very hard process. It isn't easy to change from being independent and self-centered to sharing every aspect of your life and self with another person. The difficulty is intensified when you're older and more set in your ways or when the two partners come from very different family, religious, and financial backgrounds.

I came from an alcoholic family and was raised by a verbally and physically abusive father. Bob came from a warm, loving family where yelling and screaming simply didn't occur. It took us only a few moments to say our vows and enter into oneness in God's eyes, but we

> Love seeks one thing only: the good of the one loved. It leaves all the other secondary effects to take care of themselves. Love, therefore, is its own reward.
>
> THOMAS MERTON

have spent more than 51 years blending our lives and building the oneness we enjoy today. The husband has the primary responsibility to do everything possible to ensure this bonding, to form lifelong ties with his wife. Likewise, the wife is to properly respond to her husband regarding these solidifications. They are to be taken seriously. The following Scriptures will help you grasp this concept of joining:

- You shall cling to the Lord (Deuteronomy 10:20).
- You shall hold fast to God's ways (Deuteronomy 11:22).
- You shall serve God and cling to Him (Deuteronomy 13:4).
- Obey God's voice and hold fast to Him (Deuteronomy 30:20.

Becoming one doesn't mean becoming the same. Oneness means *sharing* the same degree of commitment to the Lord, to the marriage, having the same goals, dreams, and mission in life as a couple. The oneness and internal conformity of a marriage relationship comes with the unselfish act of allowing God to shape us into the marriage partner He would have us be. Oneness results when two individuals reflect the same Christ. Such spiritual oneness produces tremendous strength and unity in a marriage and in the family.

Consider what Paul writes to the church at Philippi: "Make my joy complete by being of the same mind, maintaining the same love, united in spirit, intent on one purpose" (Philippians 2:2). This verse has guided me in my roles as wife and mother. It has called me to work to unite my family in purpose, thought, and deed. After many years of trial, error, and endless hours of searching, I can say that Bob and I are united in our purpose and direction. If you were to ask Bob to state our purpose and direction, his answer would match mine. The litmus test for us is Matthew 6:33: "Seek first His kingdom and His righteousness, and all these things shall be added to you." As we have faced decisions through the years, we've asked ourselves, "Are we seeking God's kingdom and His righteousness? Will doing this help us find His kingdom and experience His righteousness? Are we seeking our own edification or our own satisfaction?" Bob and I both hold this standard up whenever we have to decide an issue, and that oneness of purpose helps make our marriage work.

Larry Crabb pointed out another important dimension to the oneness of a husband and wife:

> The goal of oneness can be almost frightening when we realize that God does not intend [only] that my wife and I find our personal needs met in marriage. He also wants our relationship to validate the claims of Christianity to a watching world as an example of the power of Christ's redeeming love to overcome the divisive effects of sin.[1]

The world does not value permanence and oneness in a marriage, and much of our culture works to undermine those characteristics. But knowing what God intends marriage to be, working to leave our parents, joining, and becoming one with our spouses, and understanding that our differences can strengthen our unity with our mates—these things will help our marriages shine God's light in a very dark world.

God's pattern is monogamous: Marriage is between one man and one woman. This leaving, joining, and oneness results in a new identity in which two people become one. One in mind, heart, body, and spirit (Philippians 2:1-2). This is the pattern for a godly marriage. The blessing of these three principles is to stand before each other naked and not be ashamed (Genesis 2:24-25). Not only in physical nakedness, but also in nakedness of spirit and emotion. We are free from all guilt and shame before our mates. They are to know us as we are known by God. This foundation will stand the test of time.

Me and Her

She is compulsive,
I am impulsive.
She likes it hot.
I like it cold.
She is neat.
I'm a slob.
Andy Rooney says, "A's marry Z's."
But we are in different alphabets.
I push.
She pulls.
She says, "Down."
I say, "Up."
She is night.
I am day.
Living together is hard.
Living without her would be impossible.

AUTHOR UNKNOWN

Even in the best circumstances, the demands of daily life and the hours one or both spouses work outside the home take their toll on the marriage relationship. Couples become business partners, and then they become strangers. Children become the main topic of conversation and the primary focus of prayers. Elderly parents need care, bills need to be paid, the Sunday school program needs teachers, and the lawn needs mowed. Energy is gone from both of you long before the day is over, the day is over long before the "to do" list is complete, and the money is gone before the month ends. Even with the Lord as the foundation, marriage takes effort.

The Way of the World

Marriage is made even harder these days by the world's view of men, women, marriage, and family. What the world preaches certainly isn't what God had in mind when He made us in His image, instituted marriage, and declared it good.

The Scriptures clearly teach that God created Eve from Adam's rib so that she could be Adam's helpmate (Genesis 2:22). Today's society, however, slams the door on that truth. While it's great that women have made important and long overdue strides toward social, political, and economic equality, some women have, unfortunately, pushed for equality to the point of ignoring the distinctive differences God created in men and women so they would complement one another. Some have even gone so far as to say, "Who needs men?" In response, many men have become passive, quiet, and unsure about their role in relation to women. In fact, they have no idea what God intends them to be, and women are frustrated because their men aren't meeting their needs in the marriage and the family. Women cry out to their husbands, "Get with the program!" and the men softly ask, "What program?" Men and women alike have strayed from God's design for marriage, and as a result, they are at odds with their mates.

As men, you need to stand up and be counted so you can love your wife and she can accept your love. We need to dispel the lies that are given as truth. Romans 12:2 states, "Do not be conformed to this world, but be transformed by the renewing of your mind, so that you may prove what the will of God is, that which is good and acceptable and perfect." This has been and always will be the great tension we all face—that struggle of not being conformed to the world but being transformed by God. As men, you must take the leadership role in making this happen in your family. If you sit back and do nothing (as the world would like you to do), your mar-

> You were running well; who hindered you from obeying the truth?
>
> GALATIANS 5:7

riage and family will fall apart. As Joshua said in chapter 24, verse 15, "But as for me and my house, we will serve the LORD."

Faithful men throughout history have had to draw a line in the sand and say, "No, I will not cross this line. I will go no further in the world's thoughts." What are some of these lies that must be rejected? Ones that will destroy your love for your wife and family.

Lie 1: You Can Have It All

As a couple you must come together in agreement that life wasn't made to have "it all." There are times when we must say no. The price is too much. You and your mate may be very capable in what you do, but trying to have everything and be everything to everyone is too big of a price to pay. It may be too big of a risk, too many hours away from each other, the financial cost may be too great, the emotional and physical toll astronomical. Each couple has to decide when enough is enough.

As men you are the protectors of your family. The trade off of having more money is less family time. Even though the world tells us we can have it all, if you have a transformed mind, you know you can't. Your priorities are different.

Lie 2: Men and Women Are Fundamentally the Same

Clinical studies show consistently different play patterns between young boys and girls, but we don't need sociologists and psychologists to point that out. Our own observations of the world around us and contact with members of the opposite sex reveal that males and females have different priorities, think different thoughts, and have different desires in life. The differences between men and women are one reason why marriage is challenging. Unfortunately many couples have refused to acknowledge these differences in their quest for liberation from traditional roles. Don't be misled to believe that your wife's ways are your ways, her thoughts are your thoughts, and her emotions are your emotions.

My marriage would be in a heap of trouble if I expected that my Bob would respond the same as I do. Note that different *does not* imply better or worse, superior or inferior. Acknowledging that there are differences may help you and your wife become more comfortable with your gender.

> He has not promised we will never feel lonely, but He has promised that in Him we will never be alone. He has not promised that we will be free from pain and sorrow, but He has promised He will be our help, our strength, our everlasting peace. No matter what happens in our lives, we can believe fully in His promise. We can rest confidently in His love.
>
> AUTHOR UNKNOWN

Lie 3: Men and Women View Sex the Same Way

One basic difference between men and women is the way they approach and enjoy sex—and some of those differences are not hard to understand. First, the potential consequence of sexual intercourse—bearing a new life—have far greater ramifications in the life of a woman. In addition, the connection between sex and love is much closer and more important to women than it is to men. The sexual revolution attempted to erase this difference; in their effort to achieve equality with men, many sexually active women have tried to ignore their fundamental emotional needs. They have sacrificed their lives based on the lie that they should approach sex just as men do.

If more women accepted that their Creator made them different from men, they could find wholeness, peace, and a more satisfying sexuality. Often women will ask, "How can I be more feminine?" My usual response is, "By being less masculine!" Men like the softness of a woman—her chin, her voice, her dress, her manners, her social graces, and the way she relates to them.

Men are motivated sexually by sight. However, women are motivated sexually by kindness, softness, respect, and communication. For you, sex plays a large part in reflecting that your wife loves you. But for your wife, communication—talking, saying sweet words in her ears and heart—is a big stimulus for her to be sexually engaged.

Express Your Love

Take your wife out for dessert this week.
Tell her how sweet your love is for her.

Lie 4: Speaking Your Mind Is Better Than Listening

Men and women alike miss out on the bond that compassionate listening can forge between them. One way in which a woman feels loved is when her husband puts down the newspaper, turns off the TV, and gives her his full attention. And, men, she doesn't always expect or want you to solve the problems she mentions. She just wants to know that you care enough to listen.

Men, remember that women speak approximately 25,000 words a day, and men usually speak half of her total: 12,500. A woman's love gauge needs to talk and talk and talk and have you listen, listen, listen. Yes, I know men want just the facts, to get to the bottom line, to not hear every detail—but women must talk it out.

In the New Testament, James instructs believers to be "quick to hear, slow to speak" (James 1:19). In today's culture of busyness, many of us are more comfortable doing instead of being; consequently, we like to speak instead of listen.

Scripture tells us that our speech is to be kind to the hearer. One of the greatest speech guidelines is found in Ephesians 4:29: "Let no unwholesome word proceed from your mouth, but only such a word as is good for edification according to the need of the moment, so that it will give grace to those who hear." A guiding principle in my family is: "You never have to apologize for words you never say."

Any words spoken need to be covered in love. Am I saying a couple can never argue? No. You can argue, but you need to set ground rules when you do. One of them being you don't attack the other person with hurtful dialog.

One of the ways Bob and I have filled our speech with love is in the careful choice of words we use with each other. We like the two lists Denis Waitley has in his book *Seeds of Greatness*. He shares what words we should forget and what words we should remember in loving conversation.[2]

Words to Forget	Words to Remember
I can't	I can
I'll try	I will
I have to	I want to
I should have	I will do
I could have	My goal
Someday	Today
If only	Next time
Yes, but	I understand
Problem	Opportunity
Difficult	Challenging
Stressed	Motivated
Worried	Interested
Impossible	Possible
I, me, my	You, your
Hate	Love

Are there some words in your vocabulary you need to forget and replace with words that affirm your love and deepen your intimacy? Consciously watch your language. Communicate using positive, loving words. If your words are not edifying, switch gears in your mind and your mouth, and begin to speak only words worth remembering. Negative words kill the spirit; positive words build up your mate.

> I can do everything God asks me to with the help of Christ who gives me the strength and power.
>
> PHILIPPIANS 4:13 TLB

Challenging These Lies

Consider the impact that these and other lies have on our society. What role have they played in the harsh realities of families breaking up and teenagers rebelling or being lost to drugs?

When we believe in and act on these lies, we not only undermine society, but we also find ourselves living contrary to God's plan. When we try to change who God made men and women to be and redesign the plan He instituted in the beginning, our efforts dishonor the Creator. Despite that fact and despite the negative consequences of these lies, they still influence much of today's thinking about men and women.

Pillow Talk

- If you didn't watch TV for a month, what activity would you replace it with?

- Did you ever have a nickname? Who gave it to you and why?

- What do you think would be the ideal pet?

- Do you feel it's important that our family attend church?

- How many auto accidents have you had?

Love Gestures

- I love a man who holds me with no expectations for sex.
- I love a man who encourages me to go out for the evening with a girlfriend.
- I love a man who prays with me.
- I love a man who washes my car's windshield.
- I love a retired man when he takes his time running errands so I can get something done at home.

5

Concentrate on the Positive

By wisdom a house is built,
and by understanding it is
established; and by knowledge the
rooms are filled with all precious
and pleasant riches.

PROVERBS 24:3-4

It's so easy to be negative. By nature most people seem to go to the negative. It takes mental discipline to react to life in a positive frame of mind. As men, you can take the initiative and lead your family in a positive fashion. In today's scripture, we see there are three ingredients in making a stable family:

- wisdom
- understanding
- knowledge

We also receive a wonderful blessing with these: The rooms of our homes will be filled with precious and pleasant riches. This means that our homes will be in order, each member of our family will respect others, we will enjoy being in each other's company, and we can laugh when we want to and cry when we need to.

Wisdom, understanding, and knowledge don't just fall out of

the sky. We must make the necessary sacrifices to achieve them and accomplish our goal of having a great marriage.

God's Word offers us guidelines for building a solid Christian marriage. One principle is to love our spouses. Another is to let God be in control.

Husbands and Wives Are Not Change Agents

Many people who say "I do" think that after they are married their spouses will change. Most of the time this doesn't happen according to our schedules and desires. Nowhere in Scripture does God appoint us to be change agents for our spouses. When husbands and wives ask me how they can change their mates, I gently remind them that the Holy Spirit—not them—is the change agent. Speaking on this same issue, Ruth Graham wisely says, "Tell your mate the positive, and tell God the negative." Talk to God about your marriage. Ask your heavenly Father to work change through His Spirit—and be aware that He may change you as well as or instead of your spouse. Also, focus your efforts on the roles that Scripture clearly sets forth for you. Husbands are not to seek to change their wives. (And wives are not to seek to change their husbands.) Whenever I've tried to change Bob, I've provoked tension, discouragement, and resistance in him.

Consider the fact that as fallen human beings we have a strong tendency to do the opposite of what we are told to do. We want to touch wet paint when the sign says, "Wet Paint." Children want to test the "no" when we instruct them to stay away from matches, water, and friends we don't approve of. Likewise, our spouses may end up doing the opposite of what we suggest when through negative communication we try to change them. Discouraged—if not angered—by our criticism, our spouses may come to resent us and inwardly resolve, "I'll show him (or her)!" In such situations, we may be hampering God's work in the lives of our mates. *God,* working through His Spirit, is to be the change agent.

Through the years God has also shown me that many times my *responses* to Bob's shortcomings were worse than the shortcomings themselves. I have found myself becoming angry, unkind, resentful, and moody in the face of his shortcomings, and these responses impeded our relationship and my walk with the Lord. Even today I remember how negative I became when I tried to change him—but now I honestly can't remember the specific shortcoming I was trying to correct. I do remember, though, coming across the exhortation of Ephesians 4:29: "Let no unwholesome word proceed from your mouth, but only such a word as is good for edification according to the need of the moment, so that it will give grace to those who hear." That verse led me to adopt the "Is that edifying?" guideline for my speech. That little question has really helped me—and it will help you too.

Express Your Love

Write down at least five things you love and appreciate about your wife: "Honey, I love the way you..." Sign and date it, and then give it to her. She'll keep it forever.

Experience has also taught me that husbands and wives alike need to be sensitive to the verbal and nonverbal messages we send to our spouses. And we need to ask forgiveness for any of our improper responses. Rather than making insensitive and inappropriate efforts to change our mates, we must support them in prayer and be willing to wait for the Holy Spirit to do His work in their lives.

When it comes to seeing changes in a spouse, many husbands don't want to wait. Husbands want their wives to fit their ideas of perfection now! Are you one of those husbands? Consider your attitude toward your wife in light of this instruction:

> Do nothing from selfishness or empty conceit, but with humility of mind regard one another as more important

than yourselves; do not merely look out for your own personal interests, but also for the interests of others (Philippians 2:3-4).

We are to be subject to our mates out of fear (reverence) for God, and we are to ask God to help us love our mates as He calls us to. Here are two verses husbands need to consider:

- Be subject to one another in the fear of Christ (Ephesians 5:21).
- Husbands, love your wives, just as Christ also loved the church and gave Himself up for her (Ephesians 5:25).

Is this easy to do? Not until you accept the fact that God designed marriage relationships to work best according to His guidelines.

When both the husband and wife are submitting to Jesus as their Lord and Savior, both will be living according to God's plans for marriage, and both will be open to the work of the Holy Spirit in their lives as individuals and as a couple.

Again, the Holy Spirit is the one who changes our spouses—and changes us—to conform to the image of Christ. In light of that, we need to love and pray for our spouses.

We Are at War

Satan would love to destroy our marriages. Paul wrote in Ephesians 6:12: "Our struggle is not against flesh and blood, but against the rulers, against the powers, against the world forces of this darkness, against the spiritual forces of wickedness in the heavenly places." We believers truly are at war with Satan and his army, and they relish the opportunity to kill or maim our marriages. After all, good marriages are a testimony to God and His love. God wants us to have healthy relationships based in Him, but Satan wishes to confuse our lives so that we no longer know what is right. Daily newspapers, with their stories of murder, hatred, runaways, divorce, and death, show that Satan is alive and well and hard at work causing confusion and heartache in our world.

As part of his work, Satan may send a coworker, unsaved friend, or neighbor with corrupt advice for one of your problems. Weigh that advice to see if it meets the standards of Scripture. If the advice contradicts or undermines God's Word, then don't follow it.

Keep in mind, too, that Satan can bring struggles and difficulties to your marriage, and the solution he will whisper into your ear is "Run!" But as a believer, you have the Holy Spirit on your side. He says, "Stay!" And He will help you do just that (see Ephesians 6:10-17). When you pray to the Lord about your struggles, you may find it helpful to pray using Scripture. For example, "I pray that You, the eternal God, would be my wife's refuge and that you would drive out the enemy from before her" (see Deuteronomy 33:27).

We Are All Sinners

In Romans 3:23, the apostle Paul teaches that "all have sinned and fall short of the glory of God." As sinners, we are not perfect. All of us—wives and husbands—fall short of God's commands and our spouses' expectations. When your wife disappoints you, don't be surprised. Even though she may be a believer who has been cleansed from sin, she brings into your marriage—as you do—the human propensity to sin. At times we all succumb to the desires of the flesh, and we do things contrary to what we would like to do (Romans 7:15). We end up hurting the very people we love. I encourage you to follow in the footsteps of Jesus and extend to your wife forgiveness, patience, and unconditional love.

Finding Hope in God's Grace

Dr. Larry Crabb reminds his readers in his book *The Marriage Builder* that the hope of the Christian lies not in a change of circumstances that God may or may not bring about, but in the grace of God. We aren't to hope that our spouses will change, our businesses will turn around, or our children will straighten out. Instead, we are

to hope in God's grace—in His unearned, undeserved, and unconditional love for us. Dr. Crabb writes:

> Remember that the Lord has not promised to put your
> marriage together for you. The hope of the Christian is
> not that one's spouse will change or that one's health
> will improve or that one's financial situation will become
> good. God does not promise to rearrange our worlds to
> suit our longings. He does promise to permit only those
> events that will further His purpose in our lives. Our
> responsibility is to respond to life's events in a manner
> intended to please the Lord, not to change our spouses
> into what we want.… Certainly if both partners build on
> the foundation of hope and strive earnestly to live bib-
> lically, even the worst marriage can be turned around.
> Either way, there is a reason to hope. This reason is bound
> up in the truth of the grace of God.[1]

This call to rest in God's grace is one of the most important
messages for the Christian church today. We need to realize that
anything and everything we are going through in our marriages
is the forge God is using to work in *our own* lives, not the lives of
our mates. God is dealing with you and your relationship to Jesus
Christ. How you honor that relationship within your marriage is
to be your primary concern. As you focus on becoming the person
God wants you to be, you will see and experience His grace in your
life…and that grace will mean hope and perhaps even change in
your marriage.

Take a moment right now to ask God what He is trying to teach
you. Ask Him to show you what He is doing so that you can better
understand and accept the challenges you are facing. You might not
receive an immediate answer, but taking a moment to seek refuge
in God through prayer will give you a taste of the hope and peace
God gives. Think back, too, on past times when you struggled to
know what God was doing in your life. When did you realize the

blessings? Let those incidents be touchstones of faith to encourage you to persevere today.

Removing Some Stumbling Blocks

I also encourage you to reevaluate your expectations for your marriage. It's common for women and men to enter marriage with unrealistic or, at best, clouded expectations that came from childhood dreams, popular novels, movies, and television programs. Those expectations often result in what Dennis and Barbara Rainey call "the phantom."

A phantom, by definition, is an illusion or a resemblance of reality. One of the great fallacies of marriage is the false expectations we have for that commitment. Many times the phantoms in our lives destroy relationships. Are you expecting more from your wife than was ever promised for marriage? Does your phantom wife sound like this?

> Barbara's phantom is the perfect wife, mother and friend, always loving, patient, understanding and kind. She is well-organized, with a perfect balance between being disciplined and flexible. Her house is always neat and well-decorated, and her children obey the first time, every time. She is serious yet lighthearted, submissive but not passive. She is energetic and never tired. She looks fresh and attractive at all times, whether in jeans and a sweater digging in the garden or in a silk dress and heels going to dinner. She never gets sick, lonely or discouraged. And because her phantom is a Christian, Barbara sees her faithfully walking with God daily. This phantom prays regularly, studies diligently and is not fearful or inhibited about sharing her faith or speaking the truth to someone who may be in error.[2]

While the Raineys' words may make you smile, hopefully they opened your eyes to some of the unrealistic and unfair expectations husbands can have for their wives. Although the world leads men and women to believe they can have it all—the perfect career, a perfect home, perfect children, and the perfect spouse—the Bible teaches otherwise. Jesus teaches that we will have trouble in the world, yet He also says that He has overcome the world (John 16:33). So don't let false expectations—that ideal and purely imaginary phantom wife—keep you from learning all that God wants to teach you and experiencing all that God has for you in your marriage.

Consider, too, the wisdom of the Hawaiians. A few years ago, after doing a seminar in Honolulu, Bob and I were taking a bus to the airport on a rainy Sunday morning. Commenting on the rain, the driver stated, "Today will be a celebration for some newlyweds." Looking out the window, I saw nothing but rain and couldn't understand why the driver said that. I asked her, "What do you mean it will be a celebration?" She replied, "In Hawaii, we say that rain on your wedding day is cause to celebrate." I thought, *In California, rain on a wedding day wouldn't be a cause for celebration—it would be a disaster.* People want and demand perfection. We need to learn to live with imperfection. No one is perfect.

Living with Purpose

Imperfection in the world—in our homes, our spouses, and ourselves—is easier to live with when we are reaching for something greater than anything this world can offer. What are you reaching for as a couple? What is your purpose in life? Have you and your wife selected a scripture that helps you clarify or express your purpose in life? If you haven't thought about this, why not do so now? God's living Word has truth, guidance, and hope for you! Find a verse that will bring those to you, and let it serve as a purpose statement for your life.

Bob and I have chosen Matthew 6:33 as our theme: "Seek first His kingdom and His righteousness, and all these things will be added to you." In all our decisions, Bob and I ask: "Are we seeking first God's kingdom and His righteousness?" Through the years, this verse has given us direction and purpose. We also use this as our motto: Say no to the good things in life and save our yeses for the best.

In my book *Survival for Busy Women* and Bob's book *500 Helpful Hints for Husbands* we explain how to develop long- and short-range goals based on your purpose statement so you can meet that purpose. When you have set forth specific goals to help you fulfill your purpose in life, you can more easily determine your priorities. If certain activities or opportunities don't help you reach your goals for your life in general and your marriage in particular, say, "No, thank you."

Living life with purpose can change despair to hope, and hope will give you joy even when life is difficult. Living with a purpose rooted in God's truth will also help you experience more fully His grace that saved you and can make you generous, humble, kind, considerate, patient, wise, and loving. Your marriage will thrive as you work toward mutual goals.

Surviving the "Tunnel of Chaos"

Do you want to experience the hope of God's grace, remove from your marriage unrealistic expectations and demands for perfection, and live with a purpose that is more important than the irritations of day-to-day life? Do you feel that getting there seems too risky?

Author and pastor Bill Hybels shares with his readers some ideas about moving toward open, honest, and authentic relationships. Bill explains that the call to truth and authenticity must have greater value than simply maintaining peace in the relationship. This call to truth challenges us to address and resolve misunderstandings, share feelings, talk through offenses, and deal with doubts about each other's integrity. Hybels calls this going through the "tunnel of chaos." This tunnel is where "hurts are unburied, hostilities revealed and tough questions asked." When misunderstandings are not resolved, relationships deteriorate. In Hybels' words, "The secret agendas of hurt and misunderstanding lead to detachment, distrust, and bitterness. Feelings of love begin to die. It's the story of too many marriages, family relationships, and friend-ships...No matter how unpleasant the tunnel of chaos is, there's no other route to authentic relationships." [3]

> Love cannot be forced; love cannot be coaxed and teased. It comes out of Heaven unasked and unsought.
>
> PEARL BUCK

When we truly want the peace that awaits on the other side of the tunnel and are willing to deal with the chaos in the tunnel, then we are ready to move ahead. The risks are real and the work is difficult, but the rewards of an authentic relationship are worth the treacherous journey. Inside the chaos tunnel, explosions happen, rocks fall, lights go out, horns blow, and people shout—but what a beautiful sunlit morning awaits on the other side.

Are you standing at the mouth of the tunnel today, wanting what is on the other side but afraid to enter? Recall for a moment your wedding vows, those promises you made to your wife and to God. Being true to those vows will cost you, but God's rewards for such obedience will be great blessing.

My message has been very simple. To live well we must have a faith fit to live by, a self fit to live with, and a work fit to live for—something to which we can give ourselves and thus get ourselves off our hands. We cannot tell what may happen to us in the strange medley of life. But we can decide what happens in us—how we can take it, what we do with it—and that is what really counts in the end. How to take the raw stuff of life and make it a thing of worth and beauty—that is the test of living. Life is an adventure of faith, if we are to be victors over it, not victims of it. Faith in the God above us, faith in the little infinite soul within us, faith in life and in our fellow souls—without faith, the plus quality, we cannot really live.

JOSEPH FORT NEWTON

Pillow Talk

- If you could leave out one day of your life, which day would it be?

- Tell about the moment you first realized you were in love with your wife.

- What hobby would you pursue if you had all the time in the world?

- How important are your parents' feelings in your marriage relationship?

- Tell about a time when you were sick as a child. What feelings can you recall?

Love Gestures

- I love a man who is committed to marriage.

- I love a man who makes me feel accepted.

- I love a man who is a good listener.

- I love a man who has a good sense of humor.

- I love a man who helps me make our bed.

- I love a man when he leaves the lights on at home so I won't have to come into a dark home when getting home late.

6

Go to the Instruction Manual

I love the Lord because he hears
my prayers and answers them.
Because he bends down and listens,
I will pray as long as I breathe!

PSALM 116:1-2 TLB

Perhaps you're surprised by the title of this chapter. Do you wonder what instruction manual there is for loving your wife? God's Word, of course. And let me assure you that this connection with the Lord is vital to you being able to thoroughly love your wife. Nurturing your relationship with the Lord is crucial to being the kind of man and husband God calls you to be.

Consider the fruit that comes from spending time with your heavenly Father. In Galatians 5:22-23, Paul writes that "the fruit of the Spirit is love, joy, peace, patience, kindness, goodness, faithfulness, gentleness, self-control." Think about each item in that list. Which of us doesn't need a touch of these in our marriages? These are the things—along with guidance, wisdom, hope, and a deeper knowledge of Him—that God wants to give to us, His children.

Finding Time or Making Time?

"But," you say, "who has time? My 'to do' list is always longer than my day. I run from the time the alarm goes off every morning until I fall into bed at night. How can I possibly find time to do one more thing? When can I find even a few quiet minutes to read the Bible or pray?"

Allow me to answer your questions with a question: Are you doing what's important during your day...or only what is urgent? Your relationship with Jesus Christ is the most important part of your life. Isn't that what the Bible tells us? Let me also share a truth that is important to Bob and me: "People do what they want to do." All of us make choices, and when we don't make time for God in our day, we are probably not making the best choices.

> So let us love, dear Lord, like we ought. Love is the lesson which the Lord us taught.
>
> EDMUND SPENCER

God greatly desires to spend time alone with you. After all, you are His child (John 1:12; Galatians 3:26). He created you, He loves you, and He gave His only Son for your salvation. Your heavenly Father wants to know you, and He wants you to know Him. The Creator of the universe wants to meet alone with you daily, and that daily communion with Him is indeed the best way to get to know Him. How can you and I say no to that opportunity?

Meeting with God

To get to know your heavenly Father, spend time alone with Him. It doesn't matter what time or where. The only requirement for a rich time with God is to have a willing, open heart. Your meeting time with God can fluctuate according to the schedule you have. Even Jesus' prayer times varied. He often slipped away to be alone in prayer (Luke 5:16). He prayed in the morning (Mark 1:35) and late at night (Matthew 14:23), on a hill (Luke 22:39-45), and in the Upper Room (John 17).

In Southern California, where commute times can be long, I know people who use their driving time to be with God. When our children were still at home, I used to get up earlier than the rest of the family for a quiet time of reading Scripture and praying.

Much of my time studying and preparing to teach a Bible study serves as my quiet time with the Lord. Even when I don't have a lesson to prepare, I take time to read God's Word and dwell upon His thoughts. And I love it when we get to church early enough that I have 10 minutes of quiet to read my Bible and think upon God's wisdom and provision. Amid the distracting talk that is often going on around me, I use this block of time to set my heart and prepare to worship. (I also believe if others in the congregation devoted this time to reading Scripture and praying for the service, they would be more responsive to the pastor's messages, and church would be more meaningful for every worshiper.)

Meeting alone with God each day should be a constant in our lives. After all, God has made it clear that He is interested in and cares for all people—including you and me (John 3:16; 1 Peter 5:7).

Getting Started

Perhaps you want to spend time with God each day but aren't sure how to start. Open your prayer time with a word of greeting. Ask God's blessing on your time together. One small group I belonged to opened the morning meetings with a song, and you may want to greet God with a song too. Don't worry if you don't have a good voice. God cares more about your heart! The main thrust is just get started. Meeting with a support group is another good way to be encouraged in developing the good habit of spending time with God.

If you are in sales and do a lot of traveling and waiting, these "open" times can be a great time to visit God.

Several men I know get to their offices early each day so they can do their daily devotions. Another idea is to purchase Christian CDs to listen to while driving to and from work.

Reading God's Word

After you greet the Lord, spend some time reading the Bible.

Jesus teaches that we can't live by bread alone; we need God's Word to nourish and sustain us (Matthew 4:4). If you're not sure where to begin, I recommend starting with the Gospel of John. If you're getting acquainted with the Bible for the first time, in the book of John you'll find God's love for you beautifully explained and His plan for you carefully outlined.

As you read the Bible, think about the words and meditate on them. Think quietly, soberly, and deeply about God—about how wonderful He is, what blessings He has given you, and what He wants you to do. As you read and meditate, you may notice one or more of the following:

- a special promise you can claim
- a principle to help you in your daily life
- a command you should follow
- a light that reveals sin in your life
- a meaningful verse you want to memorize
- comfort or insight for the hard times you're facing
- guidance for the day ahead
- hope that encourages you

Don't read too quickly or try to cover too much material in one sitting. Take the time to look for all that God has specifically for you in the verses you read.

Spending Time in Prayer

After you've read and meditated on God's Word for awhile, spend some time with God in prayer. Talk to Him as you would to one of your parents or a special friend who loves you, desires the best for you, and wants to help you in every way possible.

Are you wondering what to talk to God about when you pray? Here are a few suggestions:

- Praise God for who He is: the Creator and Sustainer of the whole universe who is interested in each of us (John 3:16; Psalm 150; Luke 12:6-7).

- Thank God for all He has done for you…for all He is doing for you…and for all that He will do for you (Philippians 4:6).

- Confess your sins. Tell God about things you have done, said, and thought for which you are sorry. We learn in 1 John 1:9 that He is "faithful and righteous to forgive us our sins."

- Pray for your family…and for friends and neighbors who have needs—physical or spiritual. Ask God to work in the heart of someone you hope will come to know Jesus as Savior.

- Pray for government officials, for your minister and church officers, for missionaries and other Christian servants (Philippians 2:4; 1 Timothy 2:1-2).

- Pray too for yourself. Ask for guidance for the day ahead. Ask God to help you do His will…and ask Him to arrange opportunities to serve Him throughout the day (Philippians 4:6).

Time spent with your heavenly Father is never wasted. If you spend time alone with God in the morning, you'll start your day refreshed and ready for whatever comes your way. If you spend time alone with Him in the evening, you'll go to sleep relaxed, resting in His care.

Remember that you can talk to Him anytime, anywhere—in school, at work, on the freeway, at home—and about anything. You don't have to make an appointment to ask Him for something you need or to thank Him for something you have received from Him. God is interested in everything that happens to you at all times.

Learning from Model Prayers

As we spend time with God, we open ourselves to His work in our hearts and lives. Then, as we see Him working, we will want to know Him even more. We will want our prayer lives to be all they can be. Do you want that?

In Scripture, we find many models of prayer. Probably foremost among those prayers is the Lord's Prayer (Matthew 6:9-12):

> We are in too big a hurry, and we run by far more than we catch up with. The Bible tells us to "be still, and know that I am God" (Psalm 46:10 KJV). Beauty doesn't shout. Loveliness is quiet. Our finest moods are not clamorous. The familiar appeals of the Divine are always in calm tones—a still, small voice.
>
> CHARLES L. ALLEN

Our Father who is in heaven,

Hallowed be Your name.

Your kingdom come.

Your will be done,

On earth as it is in heaven.

Give us this day our daily bread.

And forgive us our debts, as we also have
    forgiven our debtors.

And do not lead us into temptation, but
    deliver us from evil.

[For Yours is the kingdom and the power
    and the glory forever. Amen.]

This wonderful example includes important elements that we can include in our prayers: words of adoration, of submission to God's will for our lives, of petition, and, in closing, of praise. We can learn much from the model our Lord gave when His disciples said, "Teach us to pray" (Luke 11:1).

I have also found Colossians 1:9-12 to be a powerful guide in my prayer life. If you aren't in the habit of praying or if you want to renew your time with God, I challenge you to read this passage of Scripture every day for 30 days. Look at it in small pieces, dwell on its message each day, take action upon what it says, and you'll become a new person.

[We] ask that you may be filled with the knowledge of His will in all spiritual wisdom and understanding, so that you will walk in a manner worthy of the Lord, to please Him in all respects, bearing fruit in every good work and increasing in the knowledge of God; strengthened with all power, according to His glorious might, for the attaining of all steadfastness and patience; joyously giving thanks to the Father, who has qualified us to share in the inheritance of the saints in Light (Colossians 1:9-12).

Now read the passage again and note what a wonderful prayer it is for your wife and children. When your wife knows you are praying for her, she feels loved and secure. When I tell Bob that I really appreciate him praying for me, he usually replies, "It's just another way to show that I love you." When you pray Colossians 1:9-12 for your wife daily, you place these requests before God:

- that your wife will have the spiritual wisdom and under-standing she needs to know God's will (verse 9)
- that your wife will walk in a manner worthy of the Lord, to please Him in all respects (verse 10)
- that your wife will be bearing fruit in every good work and increasing in the knowledge of God (verse 10)
- that your wife will be strengthened with all power...for the attaining of all steadfastness and patience (verse 11)

End your prayer by joyously giving thanks to God for all that He has given you—your wife being one of those gifts.

What armor of protection and growth you can give your wife with a prayer like this! With the Lord's provision in these ways, your wife will be able to handle the challenges she faces.

I encourage you to let your wife know you are praying for her each day. If she is receptive, tell her the specifics of your prayers. Let me assure you that it is a real comfort for your wife to know you pray for her.

Know, too, that these verses from Colossians can also serve as a good model for your prayers for other family members, your Christian friends and neighbors, and yourself. After all, everyone who is a child of God needs to know His will; honor Him in everything; grow in the knowledge of the Lord; and be strong, steadfast, and patient.

Keep a Journal

You'll become more aware of how you feel about yourself, your wife, your children, and the circumstances of your life. You'll also become better aware of what's running through your mind. Keeping track of your feelings and thoughts in a journal is an excellent means of growing spiritually and personally.

Also, when you go through a traumatic event, note your feelings and the situation. How many times have you thought, *I won't forget that thought/event/feeling,* and later wish you'd written it down? If you keep a journal—during the smooth times as well as the rough—you'll be able to look back at past events and recall them as if they had happened yesterday.

So You Want More

When becoming a godly man is a priority and you are faithfully spending time alone with your heavenly Father, you will see Him blessing you with the fruit of the Spirit. He will fill your life more and more with "love, joy, peace, patience, kindness, goodness, faithfulness, gentleness, self-control" (Galatians 5:22-23). Your wife will notice these qualities in you, and so will your children. Isn't that what you'd like to see happen in your life? Here are some further suggestions:

Focus on Jesus Christ. From the time you wake up to the time you fall asleep, try to be aware of Jesus' presence with you. Bob and I start each day with a word of inspiration taken from a devotional book or easel-type flip charts we have. Among our favorites are

Oswald Chambers' *My Utmost for His Highest,* H. Norman Wright's *Quiet Times for Couples,* and Charles H. Spurgeon's *Morning and Evening.* We try to carry the message with us throughout the day to remind us of a specific truth about God or promise from Him. When you find a passage that is especially meaningful, don't be afraid to underline it, mark it with a highlighter pen, or make notes in the book margin. Books that are marked up will, in time, become good friends that remind you of what you learned in your walk with God.

Express Your Love

Write your wife a thank-you card for just
being herself. Place it on her pillow.

Study God's Word daily. When you start the day with a devotional reading, you might come across a specific point or key verse that you'd like to study in greater depth. A chain-reference Bible is an excellent tool for this purpose. The Thompson Chain Reference Bible, for instance, is available in the King James and the New International versions, and it has an excellent assortment of Bible-study helps, including an index and a reasonably complete concordance.

For your Bible-study times, consider using a Bible with cross references and margin notes as well as footnotes. These extra features can direct you to other passages that are similar in content or thought. Talk to the staff at your local Christian bookstore; they can help you choose the Bible that will serve you best.

When you read and study your Bible, use your highlighter pen liberally. (Be sure to get the kind made especially for Bibles so the ink doesn't bleed through the thin paper.) Also, take time to write your thoughts in the margins. You might date a passage of Scripture when it has particular relevance to the circumstances of your life or the topic you are studying. Make note of new understandings you gain from familiar verses. When you do these things, your Bible becomes a much more personal guide and friend.

Should you decide to supplement your Bible reading with a devotional or a study guide, take some time to check the many types available. Again, the staff at your local Christian bookstore can recommend appropriate resources for you. Consider doing a study with your wife.

Let me also encourage you to get involved in a Bible study.

Write out your prayers. A good friend of mine was encouraged to spend 30 minutes or so in prayer daily. At first he thought no way, what could he say to God for 30 minutes. After a short time he was amazed that he couldn't stop after 30 minutes. What caused the change? Writing out his prayers word for word. Every day he opens his prayer journal and writes until he's finished praying. He dates each entry and indicates what scripture he studied that day. My friend says:

> " 'Then you will call upon me and come and pray to me, and I will listen to you. You will seek me and find me when you seek me with all your heart. I will be found by you,' declares the Lord."
>
> Jeremiah 29:12-14 niv

> Praying has now become an indescribable blessing, never the "chore" that it sometimes was in the past. I cannot write fast enough to keep up with my thoughts, so there is never a lag. No longer am I sending up ten-cent prayers and expecting million-dollar answers! No longer does my mind wander when I am praying as it formerly did. No longer do I "doze off" as has happened before, especially in the early morning.

> Instead of praying to God, I have found that I am often having communion with God. God has spoken to me clearly during these prayer times....The writing of my prayers has also greatly deepened my love for the Lord, the sense of adoration I have for Him, my desire to praise Him at all times. Surely it has greatly strengthened my faith.

Are you challenged by my friend's words? Intrigued by the possibility of having such a vital prayer life? Then why not try it? Writing out your prayers may become a real blessing, and strengthen your faith.

Looking to God Each Day

When the children of Israel were in the wilderness, they depended on God each day for food. Likewise, we are to look to Him each day for spiritual nourishment as well as practical guidance. When we stand by our God and spend time alone with Him daily, we also find ourselves in a position to be richly blessed by Him. He wants us, His children, to seek Him daily and to walk through each day aware of His presence. A regular time of devotional reading, Bible study, and prayer is essential if we want to know God's transforming work in our lives.

As H. Norman Wright points out, a regular quiet time also helps us live according to God's will, not our own:

> The key to realizing the Holy Spirit's control is our will. If we are determined to do things our own way, we will continually struggle with God. We have a choice. We can live under the tyranny of our own thoughts, feelings, choices, and behaviors, or we can live under the control of the Holy Spirit. Think about it. Your choice will change your life.[1]

And let me add that your choice to live under the control of the Holy Spirit will change your marriage in good ways! After all, it is God's Spirit that grants you the "love, joy, peace, patience, kindness, goodness, faithfulness, gentleness, self-control" that will enable you to stand by your vows to your wife.

Another way to show your wife that you love her is to have a personal relationship with your Lord. That witness tells her you are a husband who wants to be a disciple of God. You telegraph that you are a man who wants to be humble, transparent, and growing spiritually. She can depend upon your decisions that affect her and your children. Her heart is happy when she hears and sees you pray.

Pillow Talk

- Do you believe that the family that prays together stays together?
- Do you feel couples should be romantic in public?
- What important contribution to society would you like to make?
- What is the most extravagant gift you desire?
- If you were homeless and without food or money, how would you survive?
- How many children make the "ideal" family?

Love Gestures

- I love a man who affirms me in front of friends.
- I love a man who shares his future plans with me.
- I love a man who loves surprises—both for me and for him.
- I love a man who remembers special events in our lives—birthdays, anniversaries, holidays.
- I love a man who barbecues so my part in preparing dinner is easy.
- I love a man who takes care of me when I'm sick.

A Real Life Story

Five years ago my Bob went to his fiftieth high school class reunion from Poly High School in Long Beach, California. My Bob is an identical twin, and the two of them were a hit of the reunion just as they were when attending the school. Everyone knew the Barnes twins. In our day twins were very rare.

This year is my 50-year high school reunion from the same high school. My Bob and I talked over the upcoming event. I was thinking about what to wear, my hairdo, my manicured nails, the new wrinkles on my face. He could tell I wasn't feeling as though I looked as good as I would like.

Bob looked me in the eyes and said, "Emilie, you will be the prettiest, youngest-looking woman there!" Now regardless of whether I will be or not, this is what I heard him say: "Emilie, I love you!" In his eyes, I'm his wife and the woman he chose to be married to for more than 51 years. *Wow!*

7

Be Willing to Walk Your Talk

*How blessed is the man who has
made the* Lord *his trust, and has
not turned to the proud, nor to
those who lapse into falsehood.*

Psalm 40:4

One thing that turns your wife on and signals that you truly love her is doing what you say you are going to. Few things turn a wife off more than when you say one thing and do another. Remember that your wife and children are listening to your words, but even more they're watching your actions. Can they trust what you say... or are your words just hot air?

You've probably never heard of Nicolai Pestretsov, but after you read about him, you might never forget him. Nicolai was 36 years old, a sergeant major in the Russian army stationed in Angola. His wife had traveled the long distance from home to visit her husband. On an August day, South African military units entered the country in quest of black nationalist guerrillas taking sanctuary there. When the South Africans encountered the Russian soldiers, four people were killed and the rest of the Russians fled—except for Sergeant Major Pestretsov.

The South African troops captured Pestretsov. A military communiqué explained the situation: "Sgt. Major Nicolai Pestretsov refused to leave the body of his slain wife, who was killed in the assault on the village. He went to the body of his wife and would not leave it, although she was dead."[1] What a picture of commitment—and what a series of questions it raises. Robert Fulghum, the teller of the story, asks these questions:

> Why didn't he run and save his own hide? What made him go back? Is it possible that he loved her? Is it possible that he wanted to hold her in his arms one last time? Is it possible that he needed to cry and grieve? Is it possible that he felt the stupidity of war? Is it possible that he felt the injustice of fate? Is it possible that he thought of children, born or unborn? Is it possible that he didn't care what became of him now? Is it possible? We don't know. Or at least we don't know for certain. But we can guess. His actions answer.[2]

What do your actions, attitude, and words say about your commitment to your wife? Standing by the commitment you made to your spouse on your wedding day—the commitment you made before God and many witnesses—is key to a successful marriage.

Commitment to God and to Your Spouse

Picture again Sergeant Pestretsov kneeling by the side of his wife's lifeless body. That level of commitment—not wanting to leave the woman to whom he'd pledged his life even when his very life was at stake—is a powerful illustration of Paul's words to husbands in Ephesus and everywhere: "Love your wives, just as Christ also loved the church and gave Himself up for her" (Ephesians 5:25). We who are married are to be as committed to our spouses as Christ is committed to the church He died for. In fact, as Christians, our marriages are to be witnesses of Christ's love and grace to a watching world. Clearly marriage is not an institution to be entered into casually.

In light of the commitment God expects in a marriage relationship,

Bob and I take very seriously the premarital counseling we do. For instance, we never encourage two people to get married if one is a Christian and the other is not (2 Corinthians 6:14). A marriage needs to be rooted in each partner's commitment to love and serve the Lord or the union will be divided from the start because the two people look in different directions. Besides, only a Christian marriage will result in a Christian home, and only a Christian home can glorify God and be a witness to the world.

Bob and I met on a blind date. He was brought up in a Christian home, and my family was of the Jewish faith. Even though we grew to like each other and knew our relationship could grow, we had that one negative. We were of differing faiths.

> I'm going to heaven and I believe I'm going by the blood of Christ. That's not popular preaching, but I'll tell you it's all the way through the Bible and I may be the last fellow on earth who preaches it, but I'm going to preach it because it's the only way we're going to get there.
>
> BILLY GRAHAM

One night as we sat on the sofa in my living room, Bob put his hands on my cheeks and said in a firm-but-loving manner, "Emilie, I love you very much, but I can't ask you to marry me." I was shocked by his remark because I thought our dating had been going very well. I asked, "Why not?" Bob knew from his religious training that a believer was not to be unequally yoked with someone (meaning not to marry someone of a differing faith). With a firm voice he very respectfully replied, "Because you are not a Christian."

Tears came to my eyes because Bob was the kind of young man that I wanted to marry. Since I had very little religious training, I asked him, "How do I become a Christian?" At that moment and for the first time in my life, I began to consider whether Jesus might actually be the Messiah that my people had long awaited.

After several months of seeking answers, going to church with Bob, and hearing for the first time God's message being preached, one evening at my bedside I prayed, "Dear God, if You have a Son, and if Your Son is Jesus our Messiah, please reveal Him to me!" I expected a voice to answer my prayer immediately, but God waited a few weeks to reveal Himself to me. Then one Sunday morning I responded to Bob's pastor's challenge to accept Jesus Christ as my personal Savior. That evening I was baptized, confirming my public profession of faith.

As I look back over these 51 years, I know that was the most important decision of my life.

> Serenity depends on a certain mental attitude—an attitude which accepts. We have to train ourselves to appreciate the good gifts of God—material, mental and spiritual. Among all God's gifts there is none greater than Christ himself.
>
> GORDON POWELL

The Words of Commitment

Perhaps your story is not that of a happy, solid marriage or of complete obedience to God's Word. Instead you may feel very much like quitting, whether you're married to a believer or a nonbeliever. Whatever the situation, let me remind you of the vows you made on the day you were married.

When Bob and I were married, I was 17 years old and he was 22. I was beginning my senior year in high school, and he was starting his first year of teaching. Because my family was Jewish and would not attend a Christian wedding in our church, we planned a very modest ceremony at the home of a family friend.

As we prepared for our wedding, Bob and I were very much aware that the heart of the ceremony was to be the covenant we would enter into. We would be pledging to love one another even in our most unlovely and unlovable moments. We would be promising to stand with one another no matter what came our way on life's path.

Express Your Love

Let your wife be in charge of the TV remote for tonight.
Watch the shows she chooses without complaint.

Now it's one thing to whisper such a pledge in private, but this pledge to each other—this sacred vow—was to be made in the presence of family and friends. Before I took that important step, I wrestled with very typical questions: "Is Bob the right choice? Will this marriage last? Will Bob be able to earn enough money to support a family? Am I really ready to give up being single? I'm so young...are we ready to be married?"

After the ceremony, Bob and I both felt reassured in our decision to marry because we had received a voluntary and unconditional public commitment from each other. The wedding vows were a very special way of saying to each other, "I love you!"

I remember that ceremony as if it happened yesterday. Pastor Robert Hubbard had us repeat the following vows:

> In the name of God, I, Bob, take you, Emilie, to be my wife; to have and to hold from this day forward; for better, for worse; for richer, for poorer; in sickness and in health; to love, honor, and cherish, until we are parted by death. This is my solemn vow.

> In the name of God, I, Emilie, take you, Bob, to be my husband; to have and to hold from this day forward; for better, for worse; for richer, for poorer; in sickness and in health; to love, honor, and cherish, until we are parted by death. This is my solemn vow.

Those vows were made publicly and solemnly. More importantly, they were made "in the name of God." And those vows have affirmed and strengthened our love for one another for 51-plus years.

Couples who elope or marry in secret miss out on the dimensions of community witness and celebration that can so encourage and support newlyweds. The public pronouncement of the wedding vows before family and friends helps remind a couple that their marriage involves something more than just two people who love each other. Bob and I knew our wedding had sacred and eternal significance. When we made our vows before God, we were saying to each other and to all the witnesses that God is the source of our love and that the purpose of our life together is to do His will and serve Him.

After Bob and I stated our vows to each other, the pastor made this pronouncement:

> Those whom God has joined together, let no man put asunder. For as much as you, Bob and Emilie, have consented together in this sacred covenant and have declared the same before God and this company of friends, I now pronounce you husband and wife. In the name of the Father and of the Son and of the Holy Spirit. Amen.

I vowed before God, before Bob, and before many witnesses to love and cherish my new husband. Through the years, I have come back again and again to those words of commitment that I spoke at 6:45 PM on Friday, September 30, 1955. They have served as a powerful reminder of my commitment before God, the foundation of our marriage.

> Learn to commit your soul and the building of it to One who can keep it and build it as you never can.
>
> P.T. FORSYTH

In the years since that day, I have been very glad that God blessed our lives with those vows. They have been a signpost of the significance of marriage before God. They kept us together when feelings of love momentarily waned and the challenges of life threatened to overwhelm us.

I'm sharing all this to encourage you to reflect on your vows and to stand by the commitment you made to your wife. May God graciously remind you of the solemn pledge and of the fact that you made that vow to your wife *and* to God.

Marriage Vows for Today

Now imagine for a moment that your wedding is taking place today. If you were to rewrite the vows you spoke those years ago, what would you promise to do? What commitments would you make? Thinking through your promises to your wife in a fresh, new way can do much to revitalize your commitment to her. Consider the following statements other couples have written:

- My commitment to you is to listen to your concerns each day for the purpose of having the kind of marriage we both want.

- I realize that our love will change. I will work to maintain a high level of romance, courtship, and love in our relationship.

- I pledge myself to confront problems when they arise and not retreat like a turtle hiding in its shell.

- I commit myself to you in times of joy and in times of problems. We will tackle and share our problems together.

- I promise that I will never be too busy to look at the flowers with you.

- I will respect any beliefs and capabilities that are different from mine and will not attempt to make you into a copy of me.

- I will be open and honest with no secrets, and I desire you to be the same with me.

- I will reflect the Word of God in my relationship with you.[3]

Now take a few minutes to write out some new vows for your marriage. This is a wonderful exercise for your wife to do too. When the time is right—perhaps on your wedding anniversary or during a quiet weekend alone—share your updated vows with one another. Discuss them and recommit your marriage to God. These vows written by two people who now have a real-life understanding of marriage can give renewed meaning and purpose to your marriage.

After the Wedding

My friends Fred and Florence Littauer wrote the bestselling book *After Every Wedding Comes a Marriage*. That title reflects a truth that engaged couples can't fully appreciate. There's a difference between being a bride or groom in a wedding and being a husband or wife in a marriage. That truth was in our minds as Bob and I watched our two children make plans for their large church weddings. The wedding ceremony is only the beginning; it's afterward that couples face the real challenges. We knew all too well that a beautiful wedding is no indication that the marriage that follows will be beautiful.

> Real giving is when we give to our spouses what's important to them, whether we understand it, like it, agree with it, or not.
>
> MICHELLE WEINER-DAVIS

Perhaps you were caught by surprise when you first began to realize how difficult marriage can be. After all, none of us can ever really know what it means to be married until we are married. Consequently, that return from the honeymoon can be a rather rude awakening to the very real challenges of two people becoming one and learning to live together. Those day-to-day challenges test the words of commitment we spoke to each other on that special day of music and lace and love.

Tragically, we live in an age when commitment doesn't mean what it did a few decades ago. All around us and in a variety of contexts—sports, business, politics, and even in the family—we see people break their promises and walk away. A person's word is no longer binding the way it once was.

It's also possible for our commitments to be weakened by the world's message that we can "have it all." This lie from Satan encourages people to look for something better rather than try to improve what they already have or be content. Broken marriages, families, and people result when folks walk away from the vows they made to one another and before God. This lie, with its implication that we can and should always be happy, also sows seeds of dissatisfaction with life. As I look around today, I see individuals and couples who are not content with their lives. The apostle Paul shows us the way though. He learned to be content no matter what his circumstances—and his circumstances were sometimes very difficult (Philippians 4:11). Paul knew beatings, stonings, imprisonment, shipwreck, hunger, sleeplessness, cold, and danger from rivers, robbers, and false brethren (2 Corinthians 11:23-27). Paul's commitment to the Lord kept him strong despite the hardships. Your commitment to the Lord spoken in your wedding vows can keep you strong in your marriage.

Paul knew God to be the source of real staying power and true contentment, and we must turn to God too as we face the unfairness, evil, and hardship of the world. We can be content in Christ despite the hunger, wars, killings, disease, earthquakes, tornadoes, hurricanes, floods, fires, robberies, and social and civil injustices of our fallen world. Closer to home, we can be content in Christ despite the challenges, demands, and even empty times of marriage. Paul proclaimed, "I can do all things through Him who strengthens me" (Philippians 4:13). You can claim that promise from God for yourself in your marriage. The God before whom you vowed to love your wife will enable you to stand by her.

> I like not only to be loved, but to be told that I am loved; the realm of silence is large enough beyond the grave.
>
> GEORGE ELIOT

Express Your Love

Open car doors for your wife as gestures of respect and love.

Susannah Wesley, the mother of eighteenth-century evangelists John and Charles Wesley, once observed, "There are two things to do about the gospel—believe it and behave it." The easier part is to believe it; the harder part is to behave it. And that may be true of your wedding vows. The easier part is to believe the promises you made; the harder part is to act on those promises. When we do act on those promises, however, we show the world how much we believe in the gospel and in our marriage vows.

Marriage—with its stresses, trials, and inescapable closeness to another person—is certainly a test to see how we live out the gospel. In marriage we have every opportunity to share the fruit of the Spirit with our spouses. All that God asks us to do and be as His son or daughter can be—and should be—lived within the marriage relationship.

When we honor our vows, marriage can indeed be a wonderful blessing. Consider George Eliot's perspective on the marriage union:

> What greater thing is there for two human souls than to feel that they are joined for life—to strengthen each other in all labor, to rest in each other in all sorrow, to minister to each other in all pain, to be one with each other in silent unspeakable memories at the moment of the last parting.[5]

May God help you believe these words anew, and may He richly bless you as you live them out.

Pillow Talk

- What are your most secret ambitions?
- What do you think is the ideal retirement lifestyle?
- Do you feel your parents were too strict or too lenient?
- If you were to inherit one million dollars, how would you spend it? What would you buy first?
- What would you most like to be remembered for?
- Who is no longer living that you would most like to spend a day with?

Love Gestures

- I love a man who helps me with housekeeping chores.
- I love a man who prays for me.
- I love a man who encourages me to have friends.
- I love a man who loves my gray hair and no make-up face.
- I love a man when he comes up to me and wants a kiss for no special reason.
- I love a man who enjoys planting my favorite flowers.

8

Women Love to Be Loved

*"For I know the plans I have for
you," declares the* LORD,
*"plans to prosper you and not
to harm you, plans to give you
hope and a future."*

JEREMIAH 29:11 NIV

Women love to be in the presence of a manly man. Such a man makes women feel more feminine, more self-confident, and more relaxed. You don't have to be macho, have tattoos, ride a Harley Davidson, or have body-building muscles. Women love what's inside more than what's outside. A godly woman prizes leadership, steadfastness, dependability, good character, and one who lets God do the directing.

A gentle man who is strong when he has to be, has tranquility, shares the fruit of the Spirit with people—these qualities are a direct result of his relationship with God. When a man is right with God, he doesn't feel any need to prove himself. If he is confident in himself and aware of his God-given strengths, he doesn't feel compelled to use his strength to control other people. He enjoys an inner contentment that isn't based on accomplishments, status, bank account, title, authority, power, or people's opinions.

Are you this kind of man? Or are you afraid to be gentle because others might consider you unmanly? Consider this:

> You husbands in the same way, live with your wives in an understanding way, as with someone weaker, since she is a woman; and show her honor as a fellow heir of the grace of life, so that your prayers will not be hindered (1 Peter 3:7).

The husband who fails to give his wife due consideration can hardly pray sincerely with her. It takes a clear conscience before he can approach his wife for truly mutual prayer. Godly women love men who take spiritual leadership and make time to pray together. If you want to pray with your wife but have never taken the initiative to do so, begin today. Bob and I don't use our prayer time together to try to outdo each other in how eloquent we can be. Many times we take turns praying in single words or short phrases: the war in Iraq, our grandchildren, our president, our pastor, good health, safety, our children and in-laws. We finish with "in Jesus' name, amen." Some of our most precious times together are when we pray together.

Being Manly and Gentle

Most men have difficulty expressing love. Truly, marriage is very hard work, the exacting kind of work that makes us look under a magnifying glass which shows all of our blemishes and imperfections.

Women are truly unique and are very difficult for men to understand. One leading psychoanalyst stated, "Despite my thirty years of research into feminine soul, I have not yet been able to answer... the great question...What does a woman want?"[1] A good friend of mine related this true story from her family's life:

> My father bought my mother a new iron for Christmas. We had little money, and Dad knew my mother was constantly burning holes in his shirts because her old dented iron had no controls. When my mother opened up her

present that Christmas and saw it was an iron, she burst into tears.

As a child, I didn't understand why she didn't like an iron she really needed. My dad also was stunned by her reaction. Mom wouldn't say a word, but we opened the next few presents in silence. Our Christmas excitement was ruined.

That night after the store was closed and we children were all in bed, I heard my dad ask my mom, "Now, Katie, what was all this fuss about?" Mom cried again. She hardly ever cried, so I sat up and listened.

"Are we so poor you couldn't buy me a real present?" my mother asked.

"I thought you'd like an iron that wouldn't burn," Dad said. "You've been complaining about the old iron for a long time. I thought you'd be happy with an iron."

"I was hoping for a real present this year," Mom sobbed. "Something soft and pretty, like maybe a blouse."

Dad told me later, "I'll never understand women. You buy them what they've been complaining about, and they cry for something they don't need."

From then on, Dad and I bought Mom's Christmas present together. We didn't consider what she needed; we just bought something impractical and pretty.[2]

Men, don't buy your wife appliances or other "business-related" items for presents. These are "household" purchases, not "personal" presents. (The exception is if she specifically asks for an item.)

Because men are confused trying to figure out what women want, they can have a tough time expressing their love in ways their wives find special. Let me help you.

We wives highly desire conversation with our husbands. Most women I surveyed said their men don't talk. But women also feel loved when their men not only talk to them, but also listen. It can be tough to find the right balance, but hang in there!

I've heard men say, "I can't tell my wife I love her because I don't feel any love toward her. So I say nothing to be safe." Ephesians 5:25-28 reveals how men are to love their wives: as Christ loved the church. The *agape* love we demonstrate is a decision, not a feeling. Each day as you wake, decide to love your wife. Don't depend upon how you feel. Feelings come and go. Stay true to your commitment to love your spouse. Even when "the feelings" aren't there, act loving.

Here are some other strategies for revealing your love, consideration, and understanding for your wife.

Spend time together. In today's hectic lifestyle, we're all on the go. Take time to be together as a couple. If need be, put it on the calendar. It's hard to do with busy schedules, but Bob and I made it a top priority to have at least one meal together each day. Often we traded off between breakfast and dinner. On weekends we often went out for such an occasion. Many times we took children along, and other times we had a "date night"—no children allowed. Use this time to talk and listen. Keep the agenda open for a variety of topics. If you want to be heard, you also have to be a good listener.

Share responsibilities. Each family is unique when it comes to dividing the chores and duties in the home. Depending upon your family structure and if you both are working outside the home, you might need to do things around the home that weren't generally done by yesteryear husbands (washing dishes, folding clothes, grocery shopping, helping the children with homework, sharing the bedtime routine with the children).

Wives feel loved when their husbands help out. Don't wait to be asked. You get a lot more brownie points if you volunteer. Ask your wife, "Honey, is there anything I can do for you?" After you complete your help, look your wife in the eye and say, "Just another way to say I love you."

Marriages are strengthened when there is cooperation between all parties.

The man doesn't always have to control the TV remote. Ephesians 5:21 says that we are to submit one to another—and that means sharing the TV also. Yes, share the clicker with your wife...and even your children. Kids learn proper manners and consideration by what they see more than what they hear. You show great love for your wife and family when you don't always dictate or expect to be in charge of what will be viewed on TV.

You might even try as an experiment to have no TV for a month. What would your family learn during this experiment? One thing you may note is that you (and most of us) are addicted to TV. During this no TV period, introduce the values of getting to know each other better, reading, listening to music, playing games, having quiet times together, doing homework. Try it. You might like what it does to your family.

Make a commitment to marriage. When Bob and I got married, the word *commitment* meant what it said. For your marriage to be successful, the two of you must be dedicated to this institution. You both must be sold on this biblical idea.

If you both are not committed to making your union work, you won't be able to endure the ups and downs of marriage. When one person starts feeling unloving thoughts—and there will always be those times—there will be a breakdown in your relationship. You must have a moral framework to motivate yourselves to work through difficulties that will surely appear in your marriage.

Talk, talk, talk. Our son shared one day over the phone that he just loved this certain girl. He told us that they enjoyed talking until three AM. They could talk all night if they didn't have to get some sleep for the next day's work. I thought, *I hope they remember that if they ever get married.* That's one reason I've put at the end of each chapter a section called "Pillow Talk." It's designed to help get you talking. Not only can these questions be discussed at bedtime, but you can take them in the car and on the beach during a vacation.

You will find questions that you would never think to ask your wife. Through these times of discussion you will get to know her better. Make a habit of talking about matters that matter.

Be willing to give space to your mate. Bob and I are 24/7 friends. Since we're in ministry together and semiretired, we are together all the time. Some couples can do this with little problem and others would never think of being together that much. Regardless of your time spent together ratio, each of you needs time to be alone or with friends. I just love when Bob encourages me to have lunch with a friend, be involved at church with a group of ladies for a Bible study, or go with a friend to see a chick flick that Bob may not enjoy.

We all need breathing space. Wives feel loved when husbands encourage them to take some time for themselves. Bob often will give me a gift certificate to get a massage or a facial. That thoughtfulness really encourages me to be a more loving wife because I know Bob's on my team, he wants me to have some quality time just for me, and he is aware of my needs. His thoughtfulness delights me!

Pillow Talk

- What are three things about me you really like?
- What is one way I can show you I really love you?
- What trip have you always wanted to take?
- Where are you on your spiritual journey?
- What are two things you wish I would stop doing?

Love Gestures

- I love a man who is more in love with the Lord than he is with me.
- I love a man who will fight for me.

- I love a man who takes leadership responsibilities for me and the children.
- I love a man who shares the TV clicker with me.
- I love a man who makes the bed while I'm cooking breakfast.
- I love a man who encourages me when I'm having difficulty with the children.

The Building Blocks of Worth

1. *Accepting Unconditionally.* Total acceptance is the most important foundation in building your mate's self-esteem. Without it, your marriage rests on the shifting sand of emotions.

2. *Putting the Past in Perspective.* Contribute a positive, hopeful perspective to your mate's imperfect past.

3. *Planting Positive Words.* Your words have the power to contaminate a positive self-image or to heal the spreading malignancy of a negative one.

4. *Constructing in Difficult Times.* Weather the storms of life by turning toward one another and building into each other rather than rejecting each other.

5. *Giving the Freedom to Fail.* Release your mate from the prison of performance with the golden key labeled "the freedom to fail."

6. *Pleasing Your Mate.* By focusing on pleasing your mate, you communicate that she is valued, cherished, and loved.

7. *Doing What Is Right.* Your genuine applause for right choices will motivate your mate toward an obedient lifestyle.

8. *Helping Your Mate Develop Friends.* By encouraging your mate to develop close friendships, you enable others to affirm her value and significance.

9. *Keeping Life Manageable.* Completing the construction of your mate's self-image requires making tough decisions, knowing your values, thinking prayerfully, and keeping life simple.

10. *Discovering Dignity Through Destiny.* True significance is found as we invest in a cause that will outlive us.[3]

Knowing and Meeting Your Wife's Needs

Then the LORD *God said,*
"It is not good for the man to
be alone; I will make him a helper
suitable for him."

GENESIS 2:18

Your wife feels loved when you are willing to help her out. Don't wait to be asked if you can help—just help. Then look her in the eye and say, "Just another way to say I love you." Scripture teaches the importance of helping when needed. The writer of Ecclesiastes notes that "two are better than one because they have a good return for their labor. For if either of them falls, the one will lift up his companion. But woe to the one who falls when there is not another to lift him up" (4:9-10). In Galatians 6:2, Paul calls believers to "bear one another's burdens, and thereby fulfill the law of Christ." Again and again, Scripture reminds us of the importance of helping when times are difficult. Reaching out to help and accepting help gets our needs met and *creates a special bond* with the person we let come near.

I encourage you to let your wife come near, whether your need is large or small, emotional, physical, spiritual, intellectual, or material. A wife feels loved when you, her husband, trust her with your emotions. It is not a sign of weakness for a husband to share with his wife this way. God created the woman to be a helpmate to the man. You have a need, and she too has a need. Let both needs come together today and make both parties happy. You'll probably also find yourself feeling closer to her because you both have taken care of each other's needs.

Women and men are often unaware of what their partners need. Why are we so blind? Perhaps because some of us are looking for what we can get rather than what we can give. Most of us are more than willing and ready to give, but we don't know how to best meet our mates' needs. In fact, after 51 years of marriage, Bob and I still work on this.

In *His Needs, Her Needs*, author Willard F. Harley Jr. lists in priority order five basic needs husbands and wives bring to marriage:[1]

Men's Needs	Women's Needs
1. Sexual fulfillment	1. Affection
2. Recreational companionship	2. Conversation
3. An attractive spouse	3. Honesty and openness
4. Domestic support	4. Financial support
5. Admiration	5. Family commitment

Recognizing and meeting these needs for one another will mean a stronger marriage and the ability to get through the rocky times that come. (Since I'm focusing on what husbands can do to make their wives feel loved, I'll skip over the men's needs. But please know that I consider them just as important as the needs of women!) A wife benefits greatly when her husband recognizes her needs and does his best to meet them—without always having to be asked.

Affection

Women don't approach love the same way men do. Men are driven by their *eros* drive and can move into sexual desire even before love appears. Bob thought I would feel like him when it came to intimacy. What I desired in marriage was love—not sex. Men perceive they are loved when they have sex with their wives, whereas women love first and then think about sex. You as a man grow in your love for your wife through sexual fulfillment, whereas your wife finds greater sexual fulfillment when she is assured of her husband's love.

Men can usually function sexually on the basis of eroticism and physical stimulation alone. A man can become aroused at a selfish level with any woman who is available. It is easy for a man to engage in sex outside of love. Women, on the other hand, generally are more emotionally oriented. Though they are capable of being intensely erotic, a woman usually responds sexually to a man who provides security, understanding, tenderness, and compassion. Women who have extramarital affairs usually do so because they are angry, lonely, insecure, or generally unfulfilled in their marriage relationship.

As a red-blooded American male, you may not realize that your wife doesn't view affection the same way you do. She places more value on love, on the *feelings* of romance and affection. A wise man will slow down and make sure he is fulfilling those needs first.

When wives are lonely or unfulfilled because their husbands don't spend time with them, they will be less likely to respond positively to sexual advances. Dr. Kevin Leman's book *Sex Begins in the Kitchen*[2] captures this idea. He warns that men should not wait until bedtime to start getting romantic. He suggests you start setting the stage at breakfast with kind words and loving touches. Leave a thoughtful note, give your wife a call during the day, give her a hug, a kiss, a wink, and a listening ear when you get home. She needs more than your sexual prowess to fulfill her. She needs all of you!

A primary way to develop intimacy and affection is through language. Women respond to words of encouragement, edifying words, words that build up. Bob and I express our love by using positive words:

- Thank you
- Please
- May I
- Yes

- I want to
- I would like
- I feel
- I will

Other Acts that Show Affection

- When traveling, give her a rose for each day you'll be away.
- Place a flower on her pillow just because.
- Fly a kite together.
- Write "I Love You" on the bathroom mirror with a piece of soap.
- Time and effort expended are usually more appreciated than money spent.
- Write a song, pen a poem, compose a love letter, jot a love note.
- Give a "romantic dinner out" coupon.
- Wash and vacuum her car until it sparkles like new.
- Wash her hair for her. She'll love it!
- Call your wife from work just to tell her you love her.
- Send her a telegram.
- Cuddle up in front of a roaring fireplace (no TV, no children, no phone).
- Brush her hair for her.
- Bring home and watch her favorite video.

Conversation

You must have noticed by now that your wife loves to talk-talk-talk. Bob is always commenting to me as I hang up from talking to a friend, "How can you talk so long? What do you talk about?"

Men, one way you show your love to your wife is to talk to and with her. Remember, women speak 25,000 words a day and men only 12,500. When you come home from work you are all talked out, but your wife still has plenty to say.

Marriage experts tell us that the number one cause for divorce in America today is lack of communication. Everyone was born with one mouth and two ears—the basic tools for communication. Couples must learn how to use their mouths and ears properly for true communication to take place. Since God created

> Treat me as I am and that's just where I will stay. Treat me as if I were what I could be and that's what I'll become.
>
> AUTHOR UNKNOWN

marriage for companionship, completeness, and communication, we can be sure that He will also provide us with the resources for fulfilling His design.

There are three partners in a Christian marriage: husband, wife, and Jesus Christ. In order for healthy communication to exist between husband and wife, there must be good communication between all the partners. If there is a breakdown in dialog between any two members, it will automatically affect the third member of the partnership. Dwight Small says, "Lines open to God invariably open to one another, for a person cannot be genuinely open to God and closed to his mate…God fulfills His design for Christian marriage when lines of communication are first opened to Him."[3] If you and your mate are having difficulty communicating, the first area to check is your individual devotional life with God.

Whenever Bob and I are communicating with God regularly through prayer and the study of His Word, we enjoy excellent dialog with each other. The closer Bob and I get to God, the closer we grow together as a couple. The inverse principle is also true: The farther we move away from God by not communicating with Him, the farther apart Bob and I become.

What Is Great Communication?

In his book *Communication: Key to Your Marriage,* respected counselor H. Norman Wright gives an excellent definition of communication: "Communication is a process (either verbal or nonverbal) of sharing information with another person in such a way that he [or she] understands what you are saying. *Talking* and *listening* and *understanding* are all involved in the process of communication."[4] According to Wright, there are three elements in proper communication: talking, listening, and understanding. Let's look at each of these in detail.

Talking

Most of us have little difficulty talking. We're usually willing to give an opinion or offer advice—even when it hasn't been requested. Often our communication problems are not from just talking, but from talking too much.

James 3:2-10 states that the human tongue can be employed for good purposes or bad. The tongue is like a rudder that can steer us into stormy or peaceful life situations. From experience we know that our mouths can say wonderful words in one moment and, in the next, say something hurtful or embarrassing. First Peter 3:10 warns us to keep control of our tongues. We must watch our mouths at all times and be continually alert to its positive and negative capabilities.

> [Her husband praises her with these words:] There are many fine women in the world, but you are the best of them all!
>
> PROVERBS 31:29 TLB

Solomon said, "A word aptly spoken is like apples of gold in settings of silver" (Proverbs 25:11 NIV). Teaching on this passage, Florence Littauer says that our words should be like silver boxes tied with bows. I like that description because I can visualize husbands and wives giving lovely gifts like silver boxes to each other in their conversation. In Ephesians 4:29, Paul gives us another lesson in proper speech that we can apply to our communication with our mates: "Let no unwholesome word proceed from your mouth, but only such a word as is good for edification according to the need of the moment, so that it will give grace to those who hear." We are not to speak ugly words that tear down our mates; we are to speak uplifting and encouraging words that will bring blessings.

Sometimes our communication is best accomplished in writing. Make sure your family members get your messages clearly by leaving notes on the bulletin board, on the counter, or by the telephone. Bob and I like to leave notes of encouragement in unusual places to lift up one another: in a lunch sack, suitcase, briefcase, or under a pillow. We've even used a water-based felt marker to write messages to each other on the tiles inside the shower stall. After being read, the message can be easily washed off.

A card or letter sent through the mail seems to be more enthusiastically received than a note left out to be found. Everybody likes to get good mail. Sometimes homemade cards are a lot of fun to make and send.

Listening

Listening is a skill most people haven't learned very well. Of Wright's three elements of communication—talking, listening, and understanding—listening is usually the trouble area. Instead of patiently hearing what our mates have to say, most of us can hardly wait until they stop talking so we can put in our two cents' worth. God gave each of us two ears, but only one mouth. We should be ready to listen at least twice as much as we speak.

Listening is the disciplined ability to savor your partner's words much like you savor and enjoy a fine meal, a thoughtful gift, lovely music, or a great book. To properly listen is to take time to digest the content of the message and let it get under your skin and into your system. When we openly and patiently listen to our mates, we truly learn from them. The following questions will help you probe your personal listening attitudes and habits.

1. *Have you already stopped listening?* For some couples, one or both partners have already stopped listening to the other. They block out

everything their mates say by hiding behind a newspaper or working long and late. If you find yourself shouting at your mate to be heard, you are probably married to someone who has stopped listening.

When your mate stops listening to you, you will probably react by either withdrawing and talking less or overcompensating and talking louder and longer. Neither reaction is productive in the long run. If your mate is not listening to you, it may be because you are not communicating at a level that invites your mate's participation. In his book *Why Am I Afraid to Tell You Who I Am?* John Powell lists five levels of communication, each one deeper and more meaningful than the last. Try to identify the level you and your mate most commonly employ, then seek to improve your communication by moving to deeper levels.

Level 5 is *cliché conversation,* which includes everyday, casual conversation based on safe, surface statements such as, "How are you?" "How's your family?" "Where have you been?" "I like your suit." Lacking depth, cliché conversation barely acknowledges that the other person is alive.

Level 4 is *reporting the facts about others.* At this level you are quoting others instead of giving personal commentary. "It will be a sunny day"; "the Orioles lost their twentieth straight game"; "the score of the football game was 17 to 6." There is little or no emotion or commitment at this level.

Level 3, *my ideas and judgments,* is where real communication begins. Here you are willing to step out and risk expressing a personal opinion in order to be part of the decision-making process. You may feel insecure at this level, but at least you are willing to take a chance. Persons who are threatened at this level often retreat to the higher, more impersonal levels of communication.

Level 2 is *my feelings, my emotions.* At this level we express how we feel about the facts, ideas, and judgments expressed at higher levels. We may say, "I feel so much better when the sun is shining." Information is not enough at this level. Feelings must be shared in order to communicate.

Level 1 encompasses *complete emotional and personal truthful communication.* This level of communication requires complete openness and honesty and involves great risk. All deep and enriching relationships operate at this level. It takes a great deal of trust, love, and understanding to communicate truthfully. This level is not a dumping ground for negativity, but a place where each partner treats the other with love and concern.[5]

Use the following questions to help you evaluate the present communication in your marriage.

- What level of communication is most common to you and your partner?

- What are the indicators of your communication level?

- What actions can you take to move your communication to a deeper level?

If you and your mate have stopped listening to each other, here are some helpful tips to improve your relationship.

- Realize that each of you has a basic need to be listened to.

- Listen intently when your partner is talking to you. Don't just think about your answers. Listening is more than politely waiting your turn to speak.

- Listen objectively. Put down the newspaper, turn off the television, look your partner in the eye, and pay attention.

- Reach out and care about what is being said. Listening is active participation, not passive observance.

- Move past the surface message and get to the heart of what is being said. Listening is more than hearing words.

- Discipline yourself to listen. Listening doesn't come naturally or easily to any of us. Most of us are more comfortable when we are in control and speaking.

- Receive and process the message sent. Try to understand what is being said. At times the message may be painful, but you will be stretched if you continue to listen.

Timing is an important element in the success of communication. Honor your mate by selecting the best times to talk, listen, and understand. I always allowed Bob the first 15 to 30 minutes after he arrived home from work to unwind. We didn't bring up difficult topics at that time unless there was an emergency. We also reserved mealtimes for pleasant, edifying, and uplifting conversation. Serious topics were saved until after the pangs of hunger had been satisfied. Then, between dinner and bedtime, we covered more serious issues if necessary.

> What a shame—yes, how stupid!—to decide before knowing the facts!
>
> Proverbs 18:13 tlb

If you have a very serious topic to address, secure a babysitter and invite your wife out to dinner so you can talk away from the distractions at home.

2. *Do you presume or judge as you listen?* Nonverbal language is often stronger than the words that come out of your mouth. Don't start shaking your head no before your wife has gotten her requests out of her mouth. Replying before she's finished talking is a great disservice because you're basically telling her that her opinions and requests are unimportant even before she has time to fully express them. The answer may still be no, but she will accept and understand better if you listen to her requests, discuss them, and then given an answer.

In order for your mate to realize you value her input, thoroughly hear her out before giving a response or pronouncing a judgment. This is especially important when the subject under discussion is of little interest to you.

As a husband, it's important to welcome the news of your wife's day, particularly when the children are young. Diapers, doctors, shots, crawling, messes, and nerves all have meaning to your wife. If they are important to her, then they should be important to you—even if they have little meaning to you.

3. *Do you touch when you listen?* Touching is probably the best way to tell your mate you are listening to her. The amount of encouragement

and affirmation that can be communicated through touch is astounding. Often no words are needed when there is a hug, a handclasp, an arm around the shoulder, or even a playful pinch. Sometimes your mate just wants to be held or caressed assuringly. She is crying out, "Are you listening? Do you care?" Your touch assures her that you are in tune with what she is saying.

4. *Are you a gut-level listener?* Gut-level listeners are intense listeners. They focus beyond what their mates *say* to what their mates *mean.* They are open and compassionate, asking in-depth questions, ready to communicate at Level 1 on Powell's list. Without gut-level listening we often miss the real meaning of what's being spoken. Listen with your heart and soul as well as with your ears.

> There is a time to say nothing, and a time to say something, but there is not a time to say everything.
>
> HUGO OF FLEURY

5. *Do you take time to listen?* Communication doesn't happen by itself. You must plan for it and spend quality time *and* quantity time doing it. If you don't have time for your mate, you are too busy. C.R. Lawton said, "Time is the one thing that can never be retrieved. One may lose and regain a friend; one may lose and regain money; opportunity spurned may come again; but the hours that are lost in idleness can never be brought back to be used in gainful pursuits." Time spent listening to your mate is time well spent.

Understanding

While vacationing in Mexico recently, Bob and I went into a neighborhood restaurant for dinner. Our waiter didn't speak English very well, but he wrote our order on his pad, looked us in the eye, and said, *"Si."* We were sure he understood our order because of his affirmative response. However, when he returned with our dinner—or what he thought we had ordered for dinner— we couldn't help laughing at the missed communication.

We may speak clearly and our mates may listen intently, but if they don't understand the message, we haven't communicated very well. There are two major reasons why we fail to communicate this way. First, when we speak there is often a difference between what we mean to say and what we really say. The idea may be clear in your head, but the words you choose to express the idea may be inappropriate or inadequate.

Second, when we listen there is a difference between what we hear and what we think we hear. Perhaps the words you heard correctly conveyed the speaker's idea to everyone else, but you mis-understood them. And every time you respond to what you *think* you heard instead of what was actually said, the communication problem is further compounded.

> The unasked-for gift is most appreciated. The surprise gift is most cherished.

One way to help your communication is to repeat to your mate what you heard, and then ask, "Is that what you said?" Whenever you stop to ask that clarifying question, you are keeping the channels of understanding wide open and flowing. This is called active listening.

How to Communicate Better

In her book *After Every Wedding Comes a Marriage*, Florence Littauer reviews what men and women are looking for in commu-nication. Being aware of your mate's general needs in this area will help you better communicate with her.

According to Littauer, men want four things: 1) Sincerity—They want to know that the topic is important to the listener; 2) Simplicity—They want to hear the simple facts and get to the point; 3) Sen-sitivity—They will open up better at the right time and the right place; and 4) Stability—They want to keep their composure and not fall apart during communication.

Women have four different wants: 1) Attention—They want their mate's full attention when they speak; 2) Agreement—They want no arguments to break down the walls between them and their mates; 3) Appreciation—They want their mates to value them and their role; and 4) Appointments—They want their mates to honor the time and place for communication.[6]

Let me share a few additional tips Bob and I have successfully applied to our communication as husband and wife.

1. *Be willing to change.* If you have been guilty of hindering communication in your family, you are not locked into that behavior. Ask God and your family members to forgive you for your failure. Then learn from your mistakes and change your communication pattern. Tomorrow is a new day.

2. *It's okay to disagree, but not to disrespect.* Always maintain respect and honor for your mate when communicating your differences. Don't belittle, slander, or attack your partner, even in a heated exchange.

3. *It takes effort to communicate well.* When you decide to communicate better, be aware that your decision is only the beginning. It takes a lot of effort from both partners to grow as good communicators. Communication is a matter of will and work.

4. *Don't second-guess your partner.* Sit on your hands, keep your mouth shut, and hear your partner out, even if it takes several hours for her to communicate.

Solving Communication Breakdown

There are many reasons for communication breakdown between partners—perhaps as many reasons as there are couples. But several common problems afflict many couples. Do you recognize any of these in your marriage?

- I am afraid you will laugh at me.
- I know my opinion doesn't matter to you.
- I am afraid of your reaction.
- I talk so much that you stop listening.
- I know you will correct me or prove me wrong.
- I get too depressed to talk sometimes.

- I get angry too easily when we talk.
- I don't like serious conversations so I make jokes when we talk.
- I am afraid of the silence between us.
- I don't like it when you interrupt me.
- I am afraid we won't agree.
- I am afraid you will make fun of me or my ideas.
- I always feel defensive when we talk.[7]

If you want to prevent or repair communication breakdown, identify the problem areas and plan a program to overcome them. In some cases the barriers to communication may be so great that seeking a trained Christian counselor would be wise. Until the walls are broken down, you can't respond to your mate effectively.

Following the example in number 1, list some of your communication barriers, and then determine some actions you can take to repair each problem.

Communication Problems	Actions for Improvement
1. I am afraid of your reaction.	1. Pray about my approach. Choose the right time and share how I feel when she talks about a difficult situation.
2.	2.
3.	3.
4.	4.
5.	5.

H. Norman Wright also says that many of us don't communicate because we don't believe Christ accepts us as we are. And since we don't feel accepted by Christ, we don't accept ourselves, which impedes how we accept others and communicate with them. We are too busy trying to shape up for God so He will love us and accept us to concentrate on others.

The good news is that God has already accepted us because of our relationship to Jesus Christ! We don't need to prove anything to Him. We simply need to accept His love and reflect His love by accepting ourselves and others. Acceptance opens doors to great communication.

As I mentioned at the beginning of the chapter, communication between Christian marriage partners is a spiritual exercise. The closer you get to God, the closer you can get to each other. Perhaps you are not communicating well as a couple because you have never opened the lines of communication between yourselves and God. Initiate conversation with God by asking Him to come into your life in the person

> Good words quench more than a bucket of water.
>
> GEORGE HERBERT

of His Son Jesus Christ. Then seek out a church where you can grow in your relationship to Christ. As your communication with God blossoms, you will enjoy better communication with each other.

Pillow Talk

- Did you ever do something when you were younger that you wish you could go back and make amends for? Tell me about it.

- What trait in yourself would you most like to change?

- Tell me about a time you were very proud of yourself.

- What trait in me would you like to have in yourself?

- If you could eradicate one disease in this world, what would it be?

Love Gestures

- I love a man who cares enough to work on our relationship.
- I love a man who loves our children.
- I love a man who thinks I am sexually attractive.
- I love a man who is kind to animals.
- I love a man who is kind to his parents.
- I love a man who lets me talk for long stretches to my girlfriends.

Three Ways

There are three ways that prepare us for life's trials. One is the Spartan way that says, "I have strength within me to do it. I am the captain of my soul. With the courage and will that is mine, I will be master when the struggle comes." Another way is the spirit of Socrates, who affirmed that we have minds, reason, and judgment to evaluate and help us cope with the enigmas and struggles of life. The Christian way is the third approach. It does not exclude the other two, but it adds, "You do not begin with yourself, your will, or your reason. You begin with God, who is the beginning and the end."

LOWELL R. DITZEN

The Continuing Needs of a Wife

Strengthen the hands that are
weak and the knees that are feeble.

Hebrews 12:12

Women need honesty and openness. This need is so basic, yet many men struggle with the openness part. Why does this rate in William Harley's list of basic five needs of women? Is it really that important? *Yes!*

One of the great marriage verses of Scripture is found in Genesis 2:24, which reads: "A man shall leave his father and his mother, and be joined to his wife; and they shall become one flesh." This is God's command to you as men. With your obedience to that command, you, as a believer, receive a blessing. The blessing is found in verse 25: "The man and his wife were both naked and were not ashamed." What this blessing promises is that if a man leaves his mother and father, joins to his wife, making themselves one, then they will be transparent and open in their relationship. If the man shows commitment to his wife, they both can open up and not hide any secrets.

When the wife can trust her husband and know that they are both on the same page, she can open up and give her husband her affection unrestrainedly. Bob often tells men that if they want a great sex life, all they have to do is meet the three hurdles in these two verses and they too will receive the blessing of standing together naked and not being ashamed.

There is an old southern saying, "If mama ain't happy, nobody is happy!" Even though it is not the responsibility of one person to make another person happy—each of us must find our own happiness from within—the practical side of life is when Mommy knows she is loved, she will be open and honest in her relationship to Daddy.

> Marriage is a sacred vow or commitment that you both made before God, and it is a very serious matter to break that vow. God gave marriage to us for our happiness, and I believe with His help you can discover what it means to build your lives together on Christ's foundation.
>
> BILLY GRAHAM

When there is this kind of openness, partners can give their spouses the truth. We don't have to be suspicious of any question that our mates might ask. This transparency allows honest communication. Whatever your mate asks you, you can be honest. The *Pillow Talk* section at the end of each chapter encourages you to be open and honest and share. Your spouse has a right to your innermost thoughts. As a couple you get to know each other better than any other person knows you or your wife. When a person knows you, they know the good and the bad. That's what it means to become "one."

Women usually find it a lot easier to be open than men. Men can work toward becoming "tough and tender." I have found that when wives give their husbands a vote of confidence and don't always have a hidden agenda, the men feel more freedom to share their thoughts, dreams, and feelings. You men tend to be more cautious and hold back important parts of your lives until you feel safe.

Here's an important truth: Your wife will be more willing to go along with your dreams, plans, and thoughts if she can depend on and trust you because you are open and honest and loving. When you honestly communicate with your wife, she has security and confidence in your future plans.

A wife's emotional stability is strengthened when she can trust her husband's words. As a man of good character, your wife will become secure. A secure wife is free to love...and express that love. Present yourself to your wife as you really are. That way she will better understand who you are and what you say.

It's Okay to Disagree

For many years I thought a couple was never to disagree—that Bob and I should agree at all times. Then I began to realize that this wasn't always possible because Bob and I came from different backgrounds. We can justify why we think a certain way because of the way we were raised. The problem with this is that we both can support our respective choices. People tend to believe that the others in their lives should think like they do. But if this isn't true in real life, how can a couple always agree? Also, as I studied the basic temperament types, I soon realized that my Bob had a different temperament than I. We tend to respond differently to situations and ideas.

With this new data, Bob and I gave each other permission to disagree. We became better listeners and weren't so defensive and argumentative. With our new knowledge, we weren't as easily frustrated when we didn't think alike. It was okay; we agreed to be able to disagree. What a freeing experience! With this in place, we were able to respect each other's diversity in opinions more. I had a more loving attitude toward Bob because he looked at me in a different way. My ideas and concerns were more important.

Everyone wins in this outlook. Because of this arrangement, Bob and I are much more able to be united in one mind, one love, one spirit, and one purpose. To this day we are strongly committed to the real issues of life. In the big issues we are as one; in the lesser issues we still differ—and that's what makes marriage so much fun.[1]

Express Your Love

Kidnap your mate for the weekend. Make all the
arrangements. Just tell her what kind of clothes
to take and what time to be ready.

Financial Support

One area of a woman's security need is that she marry a man
who can and will support her and future children financially. This
is not to say that women are gold diggers, but in the back of many
of their minds they think, "Does this man I'm dating have the work
ethic that will give me a secure feeling financially?"

A husband's inability to provide the basic needs of a wife and
children can cause real marital strain. Each woman comes into a
relationship with differing expectations on what that economic level
is, depending on what her childhood experiences were. Unfortunately, many of today's couples set a standard of living far higher
than they are able to maintain on a husband's single salary.

A couple must decide if the wife is to be a homemaker, a career
woman, or a combination of the two. I've found that today's woman
feels she must work outside the home if she is going to have any
significance in life. My belief is that a wife should be a homemaker
during her children's growing-up years. Children need mom to be
home during their formative years. After they grow and leave home
the mom can have her career. There are many years left after she
becomes an "empty nester."

Each family is unique when it comes to this area of their married
life. Bob and my guideline is: If the wife has a career, the money
she earns should not be used on the basic support of the family. A
family needs to learn to live on a budget based on the husband's
income. If your wife has to work to pay the rent, buy the food, pay
the utilities, then your standard of living is too high and needs to
be adjusted.

Why do we believe this? If the wife has to work to support the bigger home, the bigger car, the fancier vacations, she lets her husband off the hook. Then he relaxes and sets a lower standard for what he needs to do to meet the family goals and desires. It sounds unfair, but the husband needs to step up to the plate and be the main breadwinner for the family. Most often, career women want their husbands

When praises go
↑
Blessings come
↓

to earn enough money to allow them to feel supported and to feel that their husbands are taking care of them and their families' financial needs. Most men want to and need to provide for their families.

One of the quickest ways of earning more money each month is to spend less each month. It's a lot easier to make more money by spending less, than it is to take more advanced classes or even work overtime. If you and your wife make a "need list" and a "want list," you'll find it very helpful. The difficult part is to tell the difference between a need and a want.

Paul writes in Philippians 4:11, "Not that I speak from want, for I have learned to be content in whatever circumstances I am." That is truly one of the great secrets of life: to be content in all situations. Enjoy life at whatever stage you find yourself. If you make wise choices along life's journey, you will be blessed by the Lord. Be faithful in little things, and God will shower you with bigger things.

Family Commitment

Most often women will have a strong desire and need to have a family. A lot of women have thought about children since they were ten years old. Taking care of a doll—changing its clothes and feeding it with a milk bottle—has prepared a woman for this role.

For men, playing with Tonka trucks, digging caves, and making strange noises from their mouths as boys haven't prepared them for commitment to the family.

A woman's greatest desire is to have her husband come alongside her and take the leadership role in developing a strong family. As a husband, you help your wife feel loved when she sees that you too are excited about this new adventure.

Five Investment Tips

Investing in your wife will prove to be profitable and will bring lasting assets to your marriage. So...

- treat her with respect.
- be a good listener.
- honor her as your wife and the mother of your children (if you have any).
- provide the security she needs.
- let her know you are on the same team.

A father has a very strong influence on his children—both daughters and sons. Research states over and over the effectiveness of a father's role in parenting his children. In the Old Testament, in Proverbs 22:6, we read, "Train up a child in the way he should go, even when he is old he will not depart from it."

When a father is committed to this task, the wife rejoices and falls deeper in love. One exciting trend that I see in young couples is how involved the fathers are in parenting. Husbands may take a longer time in becoming committed, but once they do, they seem more involved with their children than in my generation. Much of the credit goes to the more free time we have in our society. In my day, Dad had to work longer hours and had less time to be involved with the children. Often Dad left the raising of the children to Mom, who was available at home.

The old adage that families who pray together stay together is still true, but I would also add that the family that plays together also stays together. It's hard work to become a healthy, functioning family. A lot of times you have to say no to good things and save your yeses for the best.

One of the greatest letters Bob and I ever received from our son was when he was in college. As we read it and tears came to our eyes we said, "We're so glad that we were committed to our family. Every moment we spent has paid wonderful dividends." Was the effort worth it? Yes, it was, and so will your commitment be worth it to you someday.

Dear Mom and Dad,

As I sit here studying for my finals, I need to take a break and write you a note to express how much I appreciate the time you have given me over the years. I would not be here studying in college if it wasn't for you giving your time to encourage me along the way. As I think about the money you invested in my college education, I am aware of the many hours that Dad had to work to provide this time in my life.

I remember back to elementary school when you both always attended my school's open houses, many times after you had already spent a long day at work. You both took me down to the City Council one evening when I received the award for being the best athlete at East Bluff Park. I also remember you taking me down to the fire station to teach me a lesson after I set fire to my mattress while foolishly playing with matches. I know you weren't happy about that, but you were there.

Remember all the swim meets and the little league games that lasted until 10:00 PM? It got cold and foggy some evenings, but you were both there cheering me on until the last out.

In junior high you were there with your time and car to take my girlfriends to school functions. There were more ball games, tournaments, long trips, cold bleachers, sweaty gyms—but you were there.

You really gave a lot of time in high school—attending ball games, transporting me to school and church activities, and sponsoring my youth groups. You were even at the car wash when only a few students showed up, washing and drying cars until you were so tired at day's end. Both of you attended booster club meetings after the football games to catch a glimpse of me on the films making a good catch or tackle.

College wasn't much easier on your schedule. You took time to write me, phone me, and visit me. Parents' weekends at the fraternity house were great with you there. My friends really liked that you were with me. They think you're great! Many of their parents didn't find the time to visit on those weekends. I guess they were too busy, but you weren't. Thanks for all that. You were there.

Yes, Mom and Dad, you always gave me time, but the best thing I remember you giving me was your prayers and godly advice. Many times I could have gone astray, but with each opportunity I looked around and you were there. I only hope that one day I will be able to return the favor by giving my wife and children the time you so graciously gave me.

> The Christian home is the master's workshop where the processes of character-molding are silently, lovingly, faithfully and successfully carried on.
>
> RICHARD M. MILNES

Well, it's time to get back to my marketing notes. I love you both very much.

Love, Brad

Yes, there were many evenings that Bob and I would have rather been doing something other than attending a ball game or an open house. But a long time ago we decided our children were more important than other activities. Now we're glad we made that commitment to each other and to our family. If you don't take time to listen to your wife and children and care for them now, you will be forced to spend time picking up the pieces of their insecure lives later.

Men, women want to know that you are on the same team. It's easy to sit back and let your wife do all the work, but she feels really loved when she knows that you too are committed to this thing called family. Do you want to watch TV someday and see your son or daughter say, "Hi, Mom," or do you want them to say, "Hi, Mom and Dad"? If you want your name to be included then be an active part of the family.

Pillow Talk

- If you were stranded on a desert island, what three food items would you want most?
- Did you ever get into trouble in school?
- Describe your first car.
- What do you think God is like?
- How many times a week is ideal for romance?

Love Gestures

- I love a man who anticipates my needs.
- I love a man who loves to give gifts.
- I love a man who values me as a friend.
- I love a man who can be spontaneous.
- I love a man who asks me if there's something I need when he runs his errands.
- I love a man who notices that I have a new hairdo.

11

Becoming One,
Though Different

*They are no longer two,
but one flesh. What therefore
God has joined together,
let no man separate.*

MATTHEW 19:5

The purpose of God in creation is that husband and wife should be one flesh—the oneness of kinship or fellowship with the body as the medium, causing marriage to be the deepest physical and spiritual unity.[1]

How do we become one when we are so different? This is such an exciting journey! Bob and I had the same question put before us as we established our first home (a rented apartment). We were so different:

Emilie	Bob
Jewish	Baptist
high school graduate	master's degree
lived in an apartment	lived in 3-bedroom home
didn't know Jesus	believer in Jesus as Savior
father had passed away	mother and father were nurturing

working mom	stay-at-home mom
rode city buses	owned a car
never had a Christmas tree	always had a Christmas tree
didn't know of Easter	always observed Easter
didn't know about fried chicken	had fried chicken every Sunday
loved her roast beef medium-rare	loved well-done roast beef
loved fruits and vegetables steamed	meat, potatoes, and gravy man
17 years old	22 years old
still in high school	started first year teaching
nonathletic	athletic
organized	not organized
never had an animal	had dogs, cats, and horses
born in the city	born on a farm
never had a garden	always had a garden
liked Best Food mayonnaise	liked Miracle Whip

Needless to say, we were told, "It'll never work! You have too many differences that will prevent you two from becoming *one*." Boy, did we ever fool them. The odd makers said it would never work. But our faith said we could. I'm so glad we listened to Scripture rather than the words of the disbelievers. We have been married 51-plus years and have two children (Brad and Jenny) and five grandchildren (Christine, Chad, Bevan, Bradley Joe, and Weston).

If we can do it, so can you and your wife! This chapter deals specifically with taking two individuals with differing backgrounds and making them one in the sight of God.

As Bob and I encounter many women attending our seminars or seeking counseling who are plagued by disquieting concerns and questions about their relationships with their mates, we hear comments like these all the time:

- My husband says he's tired of talking at work and just wants to relax when he comes home. Why won't he talk to me?
- My husband doesn't spend any time with the children, and he expects me to handle all the discipline. How can I get him to take some responsibility?
- My husband blames me for a messy house, but he won't clean up his mess. Are all husbands this sloppy?
- My husband works late at the office and golfs on Saturdays. We never see him at home. Why doesn't he enjoy family life as I do?
- My husband never makes a decision; he wants me to decide. He says his job is all he wants to think about.
- My husband is always depressed. What can I do about it?
- Why do I get the feeling that my husband wants me to be his mother instead of his wife?
- My husband is rarely romantic and never shows his emotions. Why?
- My husband tells our sons to be tough and to fight for their rights. I disagree with him, but he says that's the way boys should be.

Similarly, a lot of men catch our ear with their complaints about their wives:

- I don't mind talking when I get home from work, but for two hours?

- My wife has spoiled the children all these years, and now she wants me to discipline them.

- My wife has nothing to do all day but take care of the house, but it's always a mess when I come home. What's she doing all day?

- I try not to go home early after work or be home during weekends. With the wife and kids home there's nothing but confusion—loud voices, doors slamming, and everything lying around in a mess.

- I won't decide where the family is to go on an outing anymore because when I do, nobody wants to go there.

- My only source of depression is that I don't make enough money or have a prestigious job title that meets my wife's approval.

- My wife wants me to be romantic and huggy all the time. But I can't waste my time doing that when I've got so many other things to do.

- My wife wants to make sissies out of our boys. She wants them to take piano and dance lessons, but I want them to be football players.

It's evident to Bob and me, as it should be to every husband and wife, that men and women are different—even beyond the obvious physical differences. And these differences are the roots of many of our problems as couples. Marital friction is not so much from husbands and wives being physically, emotionally, psychologically, and culturally different, but that we don't *understand* our differences and *accommodate* them in our relationship.

Although the world with its unisex fashions and equal rights movements loudly argues that there are no differences between the sexes, those of us who are married know otherwise. What circumstances have caused you to realize just how differently you and your wife think? What situations have brought to the foreground the differences between how you and your wife act?

Today's culture invites women to expect men to think and act as they do. In a marriage, these unrealistic expectations can result in disappointment. Do you sometimes say, "What's wrong with our marriage? She doesn't even care"? Are you sure your wife doesn't care? You may simply have come up against the fact that women show they care differently than men do.

> It is God's will in every marriage that the couple love each other with an absorbing, spiritual, emotional, and physical attraction that continues to grow throughout their lifetime together.
>
> ED WHEAT

What can a good husband do in the face of these differences? He can acknowledge and accept how his wife is different from him. Such acceptance comes more easily when we remember that God made man and woman different. We also need to be aware that some of the differences are due to our individual characteristics. You and your wife each entered into marriage with certain strengths and certain weaknesses. I encourage you not to be threatened by differences between your wife and you.

Physical Differences

The most obvious differences between men and women are physical. For instance,

- Women live an average of eight years longer than men.
- Men are usually stronger and able to run faster and lift more weight than women.
- Men have XY and XX chromosomes; women have XX chromosomes.
- Men have a greater amount of the hormone testosterone, which increases their tendency toward aggression and physical activity.

- Men lose weight faster than women due to the lower ratio of muscle and fat.

- Men have a higher metabolic rate than women.

- A man's blood gives off more oxygen than a woman's.

- Women have greater endurance than men.

- A woman's capacity to exercise is reduced two percent every 10 years, whereas a man's capacity is reduced 10 percent over the same period.

- Men are often physically aroused by visual stimuli; women are usually aroused by touch, caresses, and affection.

- A man's skin wrinkles later in life than a woman's skin.

- Our brains function differently. The male is more left-hemisphere controlled (logical) and the woman is more right-hemisphere controlled (intuitive, emotional).

- Men and women are anatomically different, for instance the man's pelvis is narrow; the woman's pelvis is broad for childbearing.

- About 130 males are conceived for every 100 females conceived. But only 105 males are born for every 100 females born.

- Men are performance-oriented in sexual intercourse; orgasm is the goal. Women are more interested in closeness and communication in sex, and they will trade physical sex for being held, caressed, and talked to.

These differences do not usually pose significant challenges to the marriage relationship, but they underscore that God made us, male and female, quite different from one another.

Psychological Differences

Far more significant in a marriage are the psychological differences between men and women. These differences are often rooted in physical differences—in the construction of the brain and the way it works. In *What Every Woman Should Know About Men,* Dr. Joyce Brothers offers the following background information:

> The fetus has what scientists call a "bipotential and undifferentiated brain," which means it can go either way (male or female) depending on the influence of sex hormones. The brain is divided into a left and right hemisphere. The left (the verbal brain) controls language and reading skills. We use it when we balance our checkbook, read a newspaper, sing a song, play bridge, write a letter...The right hemisphere...is the center of our spatial abilities. We use it when we consult a road map, thread our way through a maze, work a jigsaw puzzle, design a house plan or plant a garden.[2]

Doreen Kimura elaborates on the differences between the male and female brain in an article in *Psychology Today:*

> Sexual differences in the way the brain is organized suggest different ways of thinking and learning. The male brain is specialized. He uses one side for solving spatial problems, the other side for defining a word or verbalizing a problem. The female brain is not so specialized for some functions such as defining words. A woman's right brain and left brain abilities are duplicated to some extent in each hemisphere and work together to solve problems.[3]

If you are anything like Bob, you have a difficult time doing more than one or two things at a time. Your wife is probably like me and can work very effectively on three, four, or even five things at a time. Women can shift from right brain to left brain activities very quickly, and many times they rely on both hemispheres at the same time. Not men! You have to come to a screeching halt in the left brain before you shift to the right brain. There is nothing wrong with men. That's how God created your brains to work!

This data on right brain and left brain explains several psychological differences between men and women.

- Women can better sense the difference between what people say and what they mean.

- Women are more perceptive than men about the meaning of feelings.

- Men have difficulty understanding women's intuition, often thinking that women are too sensitive.

- Women are more perceptive about people than men are.

- Men and women approach problem-solving differently. Men are more analytical and deal with the problem more objectively. Women are less objective; they personally identify with the problem.

- Women can work on several projects at once. Men want to concentrate on only one thing at a time.[4]

Dr. Daniel G. Amen in his book *Healing the Hardware of the Soul* makes several observations regarding men and women:

> When we are bonded to people in a positive way, we feel better about our lives and ourselves. The deep limbic system of the brain tends to be larger in women. This may account for the reality that women in overwhelming numbers are the primary caretakers for children and the elderly. The larger limbic system size seems to make emotional connections easier for women. Women tend to have more friends; they go to church, and they pray—what I call bonding with God—more than men. Women have a stronger nesting instinct than men, which appears to reflect a great biological need to have their houses in order.[5]

Cultural Differences

The physical and psychological differences between men and

women give rise to several cultural differences, although it is sometimes difficult to determine where the unlearned hormonal differences leave off and the learned cultural differences begin. Let's take a look at marriage, commitment, and success in the business world.

In *Why Men Are the Way They Are,* author Warren Farrell states that men are performers who feel they must have an acceptable level of production to be fulfilled. As a performer, a man is competitive and goal-oriented. As an initiator, he is vulnerable to risk and failure and, as a result, often defensive in his relationships—even with his wife.

Long-term relationships are risky for a man because they expose his weaknesses, making him vulnerable to hurt and possible defeat. Instead of moving closer to his woman, a man will defend himself from hurt and defeat by escaping the relationship. If he doesn't stay, his wife cannot hurt him or prove him to be a failure. (Statistics show that men are more apt to leave their marriages than women.) To compensate, if not to ensure against failure in his relationships, a man works hard to succeed in business. After all, he rationalizes, if he is successful in the working world, he can buy whatever he needs to raise his sense of identity to a level he can live with, even if he is not successful on the home front. Success at work protects many men from the pain of their failure at home.[6]

A man's pursuit of success in business often produces characteristics that make him unlovable at home. When Bob was working on his master's degree and trying to get a mobile-home business off the ground, he was not always pleasant to live with. I thought he should value the things I valued (such as home-life and child-rearing), but he was busy—perhaps too busy at times—making his mark on the world. I didn't always understand his desire for success and approval on the job.

Our culture encourages this drive for success and holds up many other standards for "real" men to achieve. Which of the following ideas from today's culture are seeds of conflict in your marriage?

- The man is to be the breadwinner in the family. If his wife works, he feels he is less than a "real" man.
- Men don't quit until they are carried off the field.
- Being macho is important. A man must be in shape, drive the right car, and belong to the right clubs.
- Men must know about "men things": boats, trucks, planes, cars, sports, and so on.
- Men always read masculine magazines and never look at women's magazines.
- A man can perform sexually under any circumstances, on demand, and repeatedly.

These ideas seem based on learned cultural differences rather than hormonal differences, but it's not always easy to determine which is which. When you come home after a busy day, you have already accomplished what you feel is really important: You have won the battles at the shop, office, or store and provided for your family. You want to relax, watch television, and read the paper. Your wife, however, has waited all day for you and is excited that you are home. You're ready to kick back, but she's ready to kick into gear. She wants to talk.

And remember, talking is far more important to women than it is to men. Your wife wants you to talk when you arrive home from a busy day at work. She is waiting to hear about all the events of your day. She also wants you to hear about all the things she has done while you've been away. She wants to share in your life. It makes a woman feel loved when your relationship is based on communication and intimacy.

In her book *In a Different World,* Carol Gilligan summarizes the tension caused by the male's orientation toward tasks and the female's orientation toward relationships:

> Since masculinity is defined through separation while femininity is defined through attachment, male gender

identity is threatened by intimacy while female gender identity is threatened by separation. Thus, males tend to have difficulty with relationships while females tend to have difficulty with individualization.[7]

In the academic world, the question again arises: How much of this task-orientation versus relationship-orientation is due to hormonal differences and how much is due to learned cultural differences? The article "Sexism in Our Schools—Training Girls for Failure" by Mary Conroy raises this question. What do the following statistics say to you?

- Girls start school with higher test scores than boys. By the time they take the SAT as juniors in high school, girls trail boys.

- In coed colleges, women speak up in class 2.5 times less often than their male classmates.

- After the first year of college, women show sharper drops in self-confidence than men do. The longer women stay in school, the lower their self-confidence falls.

- Women receive fewer than 22 percent of all the doctorates awarded in physics.[8]

- A mere 26 percent of all high-school principals are women.[9]

- Only 24 percent of all full professors are women.[10]

In her article, Conroy presents data showing that teachers interact more with boys at every grade level—and it doesn't matter whether the teacher is male or female. The classroom scales tilt firmly in favor of boys, but not because teachers deliberately exclude girls. Most teachers aren't even aware that they treat boys and girls differently, yet studies clearly show they do. Here's what research reveals.

Feedback. Teachers praise boys far more often than they

praise girls. Boys also receive more criticism. The benefits? Boys receive more encouragement and more chances to improve. They also learn how to handle criticism.

Attention. Boys call out for teacher attention eight times more often than girls—and boys receive it. When they speak out of turn in discussions, teachers accept the remarks as contributions. When girls do the same, teachers tell them to raise their hands.

Instruction. When students need help, teachers give the boys more detailed directions, but actually do the work for the girls. Thus, boys learn to be competent and girls learn to be helpless.

Literature. Children's books still portray a lopsided view of the world. In those that have won the prestigious Caldecott Medal, ten boys are pictured for every girl.

Course Selection. Schools still discourage girls from taking math, science, computer, and vocational classes, according to the Project on Equal Education Rights of the Legal Defense and Education Fund of the National Organization for Women.

Remedial Assistance. Girls don't get special help for learning or behavior disorders until they are older and further behind in school than boys with similar disabilities.[11]

Yes, there are cultural differences in our schools, and these differences create tension between the sexes at a very early age.

Besides the primary cultural differences of task- and relationship-orientation, several other cultural differences between men and women—often framed from childhood—shape our role expectations in marriage:

- Boys are supposed to be big, tough, and active, while girls are tiny, sweet, and passive.
- Boys should play with trucks, guns, and trains, while girls should choose dolls.

- Mothers are more affectionate with girls than boys. Boys are fussier than girls, and girls sleep better than boys.

- Boys are trained to be independent, and girls are trained to be compliant.

- Boys are competitive, and girls are cooperative.

- Boys form small groups and gangs. Girls develop one-on-one relationships.

- Boys play softball and tell war stories in the locker room. Girls have tea parties and share personal, intimate conversation.

- Girls pattern themselves after their mothers, but boys don't want to copy feminine traits because they fear they will look like sissies around boys.[12]

Where do you see differences between the male culture and female culture causing tension in your marriage? How can understanding the source of some of the differences between you and your wife help minimize the stress they cause?

Express Your Love

Be in complete charge of your children for a morning or an afternoon. Tell your wife she is free to stay home or go out.

Sexual Differences

Our society fosters cultural differences between men and women. God Himself, though, created us physically different, psychologically different, and sexually different. Bob and I came into marriage much different in attitude about sex. Bob thought, *Wow!* But my mom didn't share with me too much enthusiasm. She thought it was the *duty* of the wife, but not to really be enjoyed. Bob soon learned that our difference was a big issue. Fortunately for me, I was married to a very tender and considerate young man. Both men and women need to be aware of the differences or we will never have our sexual needs met.

Most women are first attracted to a man, and then they move to feelings of love. Wanting to be sexual with her man comes later when she can trust him (hopefully for both it will occur on their wedding night).

Bob quickly realized that what I desired most in marriage was love, not sex. I desired sexual fulfillment, yes, but I viewed sex as a by-product of love. Where you, as a man, grow in your love for your wife through sexual fulfillment, a woman finds sexual fulfillment when she is sure of her husband's love. When Bob realized I placed more value on love, affection, and romance, he had to slow down and make sure that our sex came out of *agape* love rather than just *eros* love. Do you need to slow down? If you love your wife in a nonsexual way first, you will find that both of you will achieve sexual fulfillment.

Other ways that women differ from men when it comes to sexuality:

- Women love to be romanced with flowers, a love note, a box of candy, or suggestions of intimacy.
- They like to be talked to while making love—to be told how you are feeling, what you want, and how you appreciate them. Conversation builds intimacy and excitement for them.
- They like to take their time when being loved. They take longer than you to become fully aroused sexually.
- They need to feel emotionally secure in order to become fully aroused sexually.
- They want you to respect your body and hers.
- They need patient and gentle attention as well as verbal appreciation.

What have you learned about your wife from this discussion of sexual differences? How can you stand by her and support her despite the ways she differs from you sexually?

And men, like it or not, your grooming and self-care are important to your wife. Consider the following suggestions:

- take daily showers
- use underarm deodorant
- wear clean and pressed clothes
- color code your clothes to make sure they match
- keep your shoes clean and shined
- be and look sharp
- wear clean underwear
- clean and trim fingernails and toenails
- keep facial hair trimmed
- shampoo your hair as needed
- check your breath
- brush your teeth twice a day

The longer you are married, the more you will see that happiness in marriage doesn't just happen. Hold hands with your wife and tell her of your love. Don't take her for granted. Love with a willing heart.

Loving Understanding

Men and women, as different as we are from one another, are made in God's image (Genesis 1:27), and God called this creation good. A Christian husband and wife can be confident that God put males and females on the earth for a special purpose. To help us bridge our God-given differences, Jesus offers us fundamental guidelines for how to respond to each other. In Matthew 22:37-39, He simply and directly states the greatest commandments in the

Scriptures: "You shall love the Lord your God with all your heart, and with all your soul, and with all your mind" and "You shall love your neighbor as yourself."

First we are to love God, and part of loving God is honoring His creation. Accept what God has made: unique men and women created for a special purpose. Second, love others, particularly the mate God has given you. Loving your wife doesn't mean changing her. That's the Holy Spirit's job. Loving your wife means understanding how she is different from you and accepting her as she is. I think that one of the lessons of Proverbs 24:3—"By wisdom a house is built, and by understanding it is established"—is that a loving understanding for each other as husband and wife solidly establishes your marriage and your family. Continuously seeking to understand leads to less anger and frustration. You may still become irritated, frustrated, and disturbed by some of your mate's actions, but at least you will be growing in your knowledge of why she is doing what she is doing.

> A strong faith contributes significantly to successful, happy marriages. A strong bond of shared faith builds a strong bond in marriage.

In Romans 12:2, the apostle Paul offers another scriptural guideline for dealing with differences in our marriages: "Do not be conformed to this world, but be transformed by the renewing of your mind, so that you may prove what the will of God is, that which is good and acceptable and perfect." Our culture teaches us to stand up for our individuality and our rights. We're not encouraged to give into or accommodate another person's different views or desires—even if that person is our mate. Followers of Christ are to be different. We are to let God transform us and so blend the differences between our thoughts and actions that we become truly one.

Our Creator God has created us distinct and very different from one another. When we accept those differences as God-given and even blessed by Him, we will experience the rewards of more positive attitudes, better relationships, mutual respect, and godly character.

Delightfully Different

Bob and I have experienced the entire gamut of differences discussed in this chapter. We have learned to see ourselves as delightfully different from one another. Despite different backgrounds and all the physical, emotional, and cultural differences, there isn't an air of competition between us. We want to complement each other. We are committed to Christ as the foundation of our home and our relationship. Bob is committed to loving me as Christ loves the church, and I am dedicated to being his helpmate, respecting him as my husband (Ephesians 5:25,31). These points of agreement enable us to work around our differences in positive ways.

After studying Scripture, Bob and I realized that we were both made for the purpose of worshiping and enjoying God; that we had each been wonderfully created with unique male or female characteristics; and that we were, with God's blessing, to complement one another according to His plan. God's Word helped us see marriage afresh and to understand His design for this institution. Every question we had regarding our differences was answered by Scripture. We simply needed to study and apply the truth to our lives. As each of us came closer to God through studying His Word, we came to know each other better too. Gradually our differences and inadequacies became less effective instruments in Satan's hands to weaken our marriage and neutralize our ministry.

Bob and I had some help along the way, and this help is available to you. First, I highly recommend Dr. Tim LaHaye's book *The Spirit-Controlled Temperament* as a tool for you and your wife to

> There are many who want me to tell them of secret ways of becoming perfect, and I can only tell them that the sole secret is a hearty love of God, and the only way of attaining that love is by loving. You learn to speak by speaking, to study by studying, to run by running, to work by working; and just so you learn to love God and man by loving. Begin as a mere apprentice and the very power of love will lead you on to become a master of the art.
>
> St. Francis of Sales

work through your differences. Second, the ministry of Fred and Florence Littauer helped us examine our personal strengths and weaknesses and then accentuate the positive and eliminate the negative. Their books also helped us understand that people who are different from us—including our spouses—are not wrong; they're just different.[13] (Check out temperaments and their effects in chapter 12.) God created each of us to be unique, and our uniqueness adds spice to life. Let God use your differences to lift you to new heights in your relationship.

You Are a Mirror

Margaret Campolo shares in one of her many stories how we are all mirrors for our mates. When they look in a mirror a reflection comes back to them, and what they see is not themselves, but an image that tells them who you think they are. She shares:

> Remember how much you enjoyed looking terrible in the funny mirrors at amusement parks when you were a child? It was fun because you knew you really did not look like that. You could always find a real mirror and be sure you were you.
>
> In marriage, each partner becomes the mirror for the other.... Often a problem in a bad marriage is working like those old amusement park mirrors. A spouse begins to reflect ugly things, and the other one feels that his or her best self isn't there anymore.
>
> Mirrors reflect in simple ways; people are far more complicated. We choose what we reflect, and what we choose has much to do with what the other person becomes. One of the most exciting things about being married is helping your partner become his or her best self by reflecting with love.
>
> Positive reflecting will make your spouse feel good about himself/herself and about you, but it will also change the

way you feel. As you look for the positive and overlook the negative, you will become happier about your marriage and the person you married. This will happen even if your spouse does not change at all!...

In a difficult marriage, as in the difficult times of a good marriage, ask God for understanding and the ability to do what is humanly impossible. Jesus is our model. And in reflecting our marriage partners positively, we are following His example.[14]

What about your wife are you reflecting back to her? Are you looking for the positive so that she sees her strengths and good points? Do you bring out the best in your wife so that's what she sees when she looks in the mirror of your love?

A Real-Life Example

I will long remember an example of the powerful mirror we can be to one another. Bob and I were waiting to depart from the airport in Ontario, California, when I happened to notice two people. From where I was standing, I could see the back of the woman's head and the smiling face of the man she was with. Their hugs and kisses clearly reflected their love and affection for one another. That man certainly loved that woman!

When it was time for us to board the plane, the two people stepped aside to let us go by. Now I had the chance to see the face of this beloved woman. As we passed by, I quickly glanced her way—and was shocked by what I saw. Her face was not the face of a beautiful lady, as I had expected, but that of an accident victim. Her scars, however, did not keep her man from loving her or from showing the world his love for her. He saw beyond the scars to the person she was inside, and his actions communicated his genuine love for her. I don't know whether or not he was a believer, but he was definitely loving this woman as Christ has loved us—unconditionally.

The kindest and the
happiest pair
Will find occasion to
forbear;
And something, every
day they live,
To pity, and perhaps
forgive.

WILLIAM COWPER

Perhaps your wife's scars, rather than being on the surface, are hidden in her heart. Offer unconditional love despite the hardened heart she bears. The results will astound you!

May God be with you as you learn to appreciate the differences that exist between you and your wife. And may those differences become elements of cement in your relationship, giving new life, spice, and adventure to your marriage.

Pillow Talk

- If you could take two things out of your monthly budget and put the money in a savings account—what would they be?

- Do you consider yourself jealous? Why or why not?

- Did you ever belong to a club in school? Which ones? What did you learn from them?

- Have you ever felt you were responsible for saving someone's life?

- Have you ever been close to death? Tell me about it.

Love Gestures

- I love a man who romances with his eyes.
- I love a man who brings me coffee in bed.
- I love a man who laughs at my jokes.
- I love a man who believes in vacations.
- I love a man when he remembers the special dates in our lives.
- I love a man when he is able to say "I'm sorry."
- I love a man who invites me on dates for no special reason.

Taking Action

- Ask your wife for a list of three or four of her specific needs you can work on meeting.

- Spend time discussing each point so you understand exactly what she wants or needs. List these ideas in your journal. You might even want to recite them back to make sure you've written them down correctly.

- Rank these by priorities.

- On the next day, write in your journal specifically what you can do to fulfill her suggestions.

- Pray over this "action" list, and ask God to direct your path.

- Implement your ideas. Remember, they don't all have to be done at once.

12

The Impact of Temperaments

*Put on love, which is the
perfect bond of unity.*

COLOSSIANS 3:14

Have you ever thought about the fact that men are weird and
women are strange? I find Bob weird in many areas of his life. For
starters, he doesn't keep enough space between our car and the car
in front of us, he waits too long to apply the brakes before coming
to a red light or stop sign, he likes to run errands and only buy
what's on his list—no extra shopping allowed, he likes to get on
and off the phone as quickly as possible.

At the same time he knows that I'm strange. I like to clean
house, sweep leaves off the sidewalks, iron pillowcases, decorate our
home, talk on the phone for an hour, and play with the grandchildren for hours on end.

As if physical, psychological, cultural, and sexual differences
weren't challenges enough to overcome in a marriage, most husbands
and wives have to deal with yet another critical difference—the difference in temperament. A person often marries someone with a
temperament opposite his or her own. One reason God gives us
such a partner is to provide us with mates who can be strong where
we are weak. But regardless of the good that comes out of temperament differences, dealing with them can be tough.

As one of Aesop's fables communicates so well, understanding and accepting temperament differences is well worth the effort. According to the famed storyteller, a wise father sensed disharmony between his sons. He decided to have a conference to discuss this strife. He told each of the four sons to bring a twig to the meeting.

As the young men assembled, the father took each boy's twig and easily snapped it in half. Then, as they watched, he gathered four twigs, tied them together in a bundle, and asked each son to try and break the bundle. Each tried to no avail. The bundle would not snap.

After each son had tried valiantly to break the twigs, the father asked his boys what they had learned from the demonstration. The eldest son said, "If we are individuals, anyone can break us, but if we stick together, no one can harm us." The father said, "You are right. You must always stand together and be strong."

What is true for the four brothers is equally true for a husband and wife. If we don't stand together and let God make us one despite our differing temperaments, we will easily be defeated.

Temperaments/Personality Groups

You are well aware that your spouse doesn't react to situations, people, or life in general the way you do. The reason is simply that God made your wife different from you. In fact, that difference is undoubtedly part of what made your wife attractive to you in the first place. Now, however, these differences may be a real source of irritation. They may even be affecting your love for each other. But that doesn't have to be the case. Understanding temperament styles can help you bridge the conflicts and strengthen your marriage.

As Florence Littauer points out in *After Every Wedding Comes a Marriage,* the study of temperament differences goes way back:

> Four hundred years before Christ as born, Hippocrates first presented the concept of the temperaments to the world. As a physician and philosopher, he dealt closely

with people and saw that there were extroverts and intro-
verts, optimists and pessimists. He further categorized
people according to their body fluids as Sanguine, blood;
Choleric, yellow bile; Melancholy, black bile; and Phlegmatic, phlegm. While modern psychologists do not hold
to the theory of the fluids, the terms and characteristics
are still valid.[1]

While the terms today may vary depending on the "test" used
(colors, animals, "Type A"/"Type B" may be used), psychologists
agree that human beings are divided into four basic personality
groups: Sanguine, Melancholy, Choleric, and Phlegmatic. The Lit-
tauers' Personality Profile (which appears at the end of this chapter
and in many of their books) helps readers identify their temperament type and see their strengths and weaknesses.

Express Your Love

Call your wife and tell her you can't wait until you
can come home to see her this evening.

At this point, let me add that it is important to look at your
weaknesses as well as your strengths. We all proudly look at our
strengths, but few of us like to confront the negative aspects of
our personalities (Who likes to hear they are brassy, interruptive,
frank, manipulative, insecure, or moody?). If our goal is to know
ourselves, then we must look into the mirror and acknowledge
everything about us. Only then will we be able to decide what to
do about those negative traits.

Take some time right now to work through the Personality Profile
that begins on page 154.[2] You'll find it quick and fun to do.

Most of your traits probably fall into two categories, although
some people will have traits in all four areas. Which two classifica-
tions do *most* of your personality traits fall under?

The two most common combinations are Sanguine–Cholerics: outgoing, optimistic people who make excellent leaders; and Melancholy–Phlegmatics: cautious, introverted folks who like quiet, reflective thinking. Another standard combination is Melancholy–Choleric, denoting a strong and organized person who accomplishes much and really likes to work.

Rather than falling evenly into these categories, 60 percent of your traits may fall into one category and 40 percent into the other. If 60 percent fall under "Choleric," you are probably more optimistic, directive, quick-moving, and able to organize ideas in your head. If 60 percent fall under "Melancholy," you may be somewhat pessimistic, quiet as you give direction, slower to move, and prefer to do your organizing on paper. (A high percentage of business executives are this Melancholy–Choleric combination.)

Like the Melancholy–Choleric personality, the Sanguine–Phlegmatic will tip more in one direction than the other. A mostly Sanguine person will be lighthearted, good-humored, easy-going, fun-loving, and optimistic. If the Phlegmatic prevails, a person will have a dry sense of humor and be quieter, slower-paced, and more laid back, giving the impression that he or she is not concerned about anything. Sanguine–Phlegmatics are always friendly, relaxed, and appealing people, but they can also be poor handlers of money. Also, believing that "all work and no play makes Jack a dull boy," they feel a strong tug-of-war between the two and may often be unable to get their careers on track.

An adaptation of Florence Littauer's summaries of each one of the temperaments begins on page 145.[3] With an open mind and heart, read the two categories into which most of your traits fall. These two summaries are not cast in concrete; they merely are an *indication* of your personality type, a benchmark to help you learn about yourself.

After carefully reading through the two descriptions that your Personality Profile suggested best fit you, spend some time thinking about what you've read. What do these overviews say about you? In what areas do you think God would like you to work on becoming more Christlike? Ask your spouse or a trusted friend how accurately the descriptions fit you.

According to 1 Corinthians 11:28, we are to examine ourselves before we receive communion, but such self-examination can be beneficial at other times as well. When we look at ourselves, we can see where God would change us. We can also stop trying to change others and allow them to be themselves. When we allow our spouses to be different from us, our marriages will definitely improve.

God created each of us to be unique. Accept wholeheartedly those areas where your spouse is different from you. Learn from her. Offer your strengths where she is weak, and let her strengths complement your weaknesses. A richer marriage will result.

Personality Profiles

Sanguine Summary "Let's do it the fun way."	
Desire:	Have fun.
Emotional Needs:	Attention, affection, approval, acceptance.
Key Strengths:	Can talk about anything at any time at any place with or without information. Has a bubbling personality, optimism, sense of humor, storytelling ability, likes people.
Key Weaknesses:	Disorganized, can't remember details or names, exaggerates, not serious about anything, trusts others to do the work, too gullible and naïve.

Gets Depressed When:	Life is not fun and no one seems to love him.
Is Afraid of:	Being unpopular or bored, having to live by the clock or keep a record of money spent.
Likes People Who:	Listen and laugh, praise and approve.
Dislikes People Who:	Criticize, don't respond to his humor, don't think he is cute.
Is Valuable in Work:	For colorful creativity, optimism, light touch, cheering up others, entertaining.
As a Leader He:	Has unlimited energy and enthusiasm, inspires others, encourages participation, sometimes doesn't follow through, is easily distracted.
Could Improve If:	He got organized, didn't talk so much, and learned to manage time.
Tends to Marry:	Melancholies who are sensitive and serious, but Sanguines quickly tire of having to cheer them up all the time and being made to feel inadequate and stupid.
Reaction to Stress:	Leave the scene, do an enjoyable activity, find a fun group, create excuses, blame others.
Recognize by:	Constant talking, loud volume, bright eyes, moving hands, col-

orful expressions, enthusiasm,
ability to mix easily.

Choleric Summary
"Let's do it my way."

Desire:	Have control.
Emotional Needs:	Sense of obedience, appreciation for accomplishments, credit for ability.
Key Strengths:	Ability to take charge of anything instantly, make quick, correct judgments.
Key Weaknesses:	Too bossy, domineering, autocratic, insensitive, impatient, unwilling to delegate or give credit to others.
Gets Depressed When:	Life is out of control, and people won't do things his way.
Is Afraid of:	Losing control of anything, such as losing job, not being promoted, becoming seriously ill, having a rebellious child or unsupportive mate.
Likes People Who:	Are supportive and submissive, see things his way, cooperate quickly, and let him take credit.
Dislikes People Who:	Are lazy and not interested in working constantly, who buck his authority, get independent, aren't loyal.

Is Valuable in Work:	He can accomplish more than anyone else in a shorter time and is usually right, but may stir up trouble.
Could Improve If:	He allowed others to make decisions, delegated authority, became more patient, didn't expect everyone to produce as he does.
As a Leader He:	Has a natural feel for being in charge, a quick sense of what will work, and a sincere belief in his ability to achieve, but may overwhelm less aggressive people.
Tends to Marry:	Phlegmatics who will quietly obey and not buck his authority, but who never accomplish enough or get excited over his projects.
Reaction to Stress:	Tighten control, work harder, exercise more, get rid of offender.
Recognize by:	Fast-moving approach, quick grab for control, self-confidence, restless and overpowering attitude.

Melancholy Summary
"Let's do it the right way."

Desire:	Have it right.
Emotional Needs:	Sense of stability, space, silence, sensitivity, and support.

Key Strengths:	Ability to organize, set long-range goals, have high standards and ideals, analyze deeply.
Key Weaknesses:	Easily depressed, too much time on preparation, too focused on details, remembers negatives, suspicious of others.
Gets Depressed When:	Life is out of order, standards aren't met, no one seems to care.
Is Afraid of:	No one understanding how he really feels, making a mistake, having to compromise standards.
Likes People Who:	Are serious, intellectual, deep, and will carry on a sensible conversation.
Dislikes People Who:	Are lightweights, forgetful, late, disorganized, superficial, prevaricating, unpredictable.
Is Valuable in Work:	For sense of details, love of analysis, follow-through, high standards of performance, compassion for the hurting.
Could Improve If:	He didn't take life quite so seriously and didn't insist others be perfectionists.
As a Leader He:	Organizes well, is sensitive to people's feelings, has deep creativity, wants quality performance.
Tends to Marry:	Sanguines for their personalities and social skills, but soon

tries to shut them up and get them on a schedule, becoming depressed when they don't respond.

Reaction to Stress:	Withdraws, gets lost in a book, becomes depressed, gives up, recounts the problems.
Recognize by:	Serious, sensitive nature, well-mannered approach, self-deprecating comments, meticulous and well-groomed looks (exceptions are hippy-type intellectuals, musicians, poets, who feel attention to clothes and looks is worldly and detracts from their inner strengths).

Phlegmatic Summary
"Let's do it the easy way."

Desire:	Have no conflict; keep peace.
Emotional Needs:	Sense of respect, feeling of worth, understanding, emotional support, harmony.
Key Strengths:	Balance, even disposition, dry sense of humor, pleasing personality.
Key Weaknesses:	Lack of decisiveness, enthusiasm, and energy, has no obvious flaws, and has a hidden will of iron.

Gets Depressed When:	Life is full of conflict, he has to face a personal confrontation, no one wants to help, the buck stops with him.
Is Afraid of:	Having to deal with a major personal problem, being left holding the bag, making major changes.
Likes People Who:	Will make decisions for him, will recognize his strengths, will not ignore him.
Dislikes People Who:	Are too pushy, expect too much of him.
Is Valuable in Work:	Because he cooperates and is a calming influence, keeps peace, mediates between contentious people, objectively solves problems.
Could Improve If:	He sets goals and becomes self-motivated, he were willing to do more and move faster than expected and could face his own problems as well as he handles other people's.
As a Leader He:	Keeps calm, cool, and collected. Doesn't make impulsive decisions, is well-liked and inoffensive, won't cause trouble, but doesn't come up with brilliant new ideas.
Tends to Marry:	Cholerics because of their strength and decisiveness, but later he gets tired of being

	pushed around and looked down upon.
Reaction to Stress:	Hide from it, watch TV, eat.
Recognize by:	Calm approach, relaxed posture, sitting or leaning when possible.

Pillow Talk

- How often do you pray?
- Name your best memory of a teacher.
- What would or wouldn't you do for $1,000,000?
- Would you rather live in the past, the present, or the future? Why?
- If you could spend one day with your mother, what would you like to do?

Love Gestures

- I love a man who finds articles in magazines and newspapers that I would like.
- I love a man who gets excited waiting to see my reaction to opening a gift he has given me.
- I love a man who has good health habits.
- I love a man who loves his parents.
- I love a man who picks up and hangs up his clothes.
- I love a man who brings me home special gifts.
- I love a man who is kind to strangers.
- I love a man who keeps the rain and snow off me with an umbrella.

Don't Quit

When things go wrong, as they sometimes will,
When the road you're trudging seems all uphill,
When the funds are low and the debts are high,
And you want to smile but you have to sigh,
When care is pressing you down a bit,
Rest if you must, but don't you quit.

Life is strange with its twists and turns
As every one of us sometimes learns;
And many a failure turns about
When he might have won had he stuck it out.
Don't give up though the pace seems slow;
You may succeed with another blow!

Success is failure turned inside out,
The silver tint of the clouds of doubt;
And you never can tell just how close you are,
It may be near when it seems so far.
So stick to the fight when you're hardest hit;
It's when things seem worst that you mustn't quit.

AUTHOR UNKNOWN

PERSONALITY PROFILE

DIRECTIONS—In each of the following rows of four words across, place an X in front of one word that most often applies to you. Continue through all 40 lines. Be sure each number is marked. Then transfer the X's to the corresponding words on the chart on the next page.

STRENGTHS

1 ____ Submissive	____ Self-sacrificing	____ Sociable	____ Strong-willed
2 ____ Animated	____ Adventurous	____ Analytical	____ Adaptable
3 ____ Persistent	____ Playful	____ Persuasive	____ Peaceful
4 ____ Considerate	____ Controlled	____ Competitive	____ Convincing
5 ____ Refreshing	____ Respectful	____ Reserved	____ Resourceful
6 ____ Satisfied	____ Sensitive	____ Self-reliant	____ Spirited
7 ____ Planner	____ Patient	____ Positive	____ Promoter
8 ____ Sure	____ Spontaneous	____ Scheduled	____ Shy
9 ____ Orderly	____ Obliging	____ Outspoken	____ Optimistic
10 ____ Friendly	____ Faithful	____ Funny	____ Forceful
11 ____ Daring	____ Delightful	____ Diplomatic	____ Detailed
12 ____ Cheerful	____ Consistent	____ Cultured	____ Confident
13 ____ Idealistic	____ Independent	____ Inoffensive	____ Inspiring
14 ____ Demonstrative	____ Decisive	____ Dry humor	____ Deep
15 ____ Mediator	____ Musical	____ Mover	____ Mixes easily
16 ____ Thoughtful	____ Tenacious	____ Talker	____ Tolerant
17 ____ Listener	____ Loyal	____ Leader	____ Lively
18 ____ Contented	____ Chief	____ Chartmaker	____ Cute
19 ____ Perfectionist	____ Permissive	____ Productive	____ Popular
20 ____ Bouncy	____ Bold	____ Behaved	____ Balanced

WEAKNESSES

21 ____ Brassy	____ Bossy	____ Bashful	____ Blank
22 ____ Undisciplined	____ Unsympathetic	____ Unenthusiastic	____ Unforgiving
23 ____ Reluctant	____ Resentful	____ Resistant	____ Repetitious
24 ____ Fussy	____ Fearful	____ Forgetful	____ Frank
25 ____ Impatient	____ Insecure	____ Indecisive	____ Interrupts
26 ____ Unpopular	____ Uninvolved	____ Unpredictable	____ Unaffectionate
27 ____ Headstrong	____ Haphazard	____ Hard to please	____ Hesitant
28 ____ Plain	____ Pessimistic	____ Proud	____ Permissive
29 ____ Angered easily	____ Aimless	____ Argumentative	____ Alienated
30 ____ Naïve	____ Negative attitude	____ Nervy	____ Nonchalant
31 ____ Worrier	____ Withdrawn	____ Workaholic	____ Wants credit
32 ____ Too sensitive	____ Tactless	____ Timid	____ Talkative
33 ____ Doubtful	____ Disorganized	____ Domineering	____ Depressed
34 ____ Inconsistent	____ Introvert	____ Intolerant	____ Indifferent
35 ____ Messy	____ Moody	____ Mumbles	____ Manipulative
36 ____ Slow	____ Stubborn	____ Show-off	____ Skeptical
37 ____ Loner	____ Lord over	____ Lazy	____ Loud
38 ____ Sluggish	____ Suspicious	____ Short-tempered	____ Scatterbrained
39 ____ Revengeful	____ Restless	____ Reluctant	____ Rash
40 ____ Compromising	____ Critical	____ Crafty	____ Changeable

PERSONALITY SCORING SHEET

After transfering the X's from the previous page to the corresponding words below, add up your totals. Your highest and second highest columns reveal your primary and secondary personality types.

STRENGTHS

	SANGUINE	CHOLERIC	MELANCHOLY	PHLEGMATIC
1	Sociable	Strong-willed	Self-sacrificing	Submissive
2	Animated	Adventurous	Analytical	Adaptable
3	Playful	Persuasive	Persistent	Peaceful
4	Convincing	Competitive	Considerate	Controlled
5	Refreshing	Resourceful	Respectful	Reserved
6	Spirited	Self-reliant	Sensitive	Satisfied
7	Promoter	Positive	Planner	Patient
8	Spontaneous	Sure	Scheduled	Shy
9	Optimistic	Outspoken	Orderly	Obliging
10	Funny	Forceful	Faithful	Friendly
11	Delightful	Daring	Detailed	Diplomatic
12	Cheerful	Confident	Cultured	Consistent
13	Inspiring	Independent	Idealistic	Inoffensive
14	Demonstrative	Decisive	Deep	Dry humor
15	Mixes easily	Mover	Musical	Mediator
16	Talker	Tenacious	Thoughtful	Tolerant
17	Lively	Leader	Loyal	Listener
18	Cute	Chief	Chartmaker	Contented
19	Popular	Productive	Perfectionist	Permissive
20	Bouncy	Bold	Behaved	Balanced

TOTALS _____ _____ _____ _____

WEAKNESSES

	SANGUINE	CHOLERIC	MELANCHOLY	PHLEGMATIC
21	Brassy	Bossy	Bashful	Blank
22	Undisciplined	Unsympathetic	Unforgiving	Unenthusiastic
23	Repetitious	Resistant	Resentful	Reluctant
24	Forgetful	Frank	Fussy	Fearful
25	Interrupts	Impatient	Insecure	Indecisive
26	Unpredictable	Unaffectionate	Unpopular	Uninvolved
27	Haphazard	Headstrong	Hard-to-please	Hesitant
28	Permissive	Proud	Pessimistic	Plain
29	Angered easily	Argumentative	Alienated	Aimless
30	Naïve	Nervy	Negative attitude	Nonchalant
31	Wants credit	Workaholic	Withdrawn	Worrier
32	Talkative	Tactless	Too sensitive	Timid
33	Disorganized	Domineering	Depressed	Doubtful
34	Inconsistent	Intolerant	Introvert	Indifferent
35	Messy	Manipulative	Moody	Mumbles
36	Show-off	Stubborn	Skeptical	Slow
37	Loud	Lord-over-others	Loner	Lazy
38	Scatterbrained	Short tempered	Suspicious	Sluggish
39	Restless	Rash	Revengeful	Reluctant
40	Changeable	Crafty	Critical	Compromising

TOTALS _____ _____ _____ _____

COMBINED TOTALS _____ _____ _____ _____

13

Being a Friend with Your Partner

Unless the LORD *builds the house,*
they labor in vain who build it.

PSALM 127:1

A husband and wife who are also best friends will have a deeper, stronger marriage. Through the years Bob and I have grown our friendship status to the point where we each say, "You are my best friend!"

God gives the woman to the man to be a "helper suitable for him" (Genesis 2:18). Take the time to list the ways your wife helps you at home and at work. Share these with her and tell her thank you! Reveal how she is "suitable" when it comes to recognizing and meeting your needs. This would be a great topic of conversation for a *Pillow Talk* discussion.

God created human beings in His image (Genesis 1:27). The fact that each one of us is created in God's image calls us to honor and respect one another. Consider for a moment that your wife was made by God in His image, just as you were. How do you treat your spouse that reflects that? How can you improve in this area?

God created woman from man's rib (Genesis 2:21-22). Adam perceived Eve as part of his own bone and own flesh (Genesis 2:23). If you follow Adam's example you rightly understand that your wife is actually part of you. You will want to treat her as well as you treat

157

yourself. You will want to take good care of her and provide for her every need. This kind of husband-love provides a good foundation for deep friendship.

A man is to leave his parents and be joined to his wife (Genesis 2:24). You help the joining happen when you show—not just tell—your wife that she is your most important priority after God. Wives need to know that they don't have to compete with your mother or any other female for the number one position in your life. She must know that you respect, honor, and love her if she is to act out her proper role as woman, wife, and mother. Besides building up your wife's confidence, your clear communication of your love for her will strengthen the bond of marriage.

The man and the woman stood naked before each other and were not ashamed (Genesis 2:25). When husbands and wives accept the first four principles—when we understand that we are created in God's image, when husbands recognize that their wives are bone of their bones and flesh of their flesh (2:23) and treat them as such, when a wife is a suitable helper to her man, and when spouses join to one another—they can indeed stand before one another naked and not ashamed. I don't think a married couple can explore the depths of friendship until they stand before each other open and vulnerable—physically, emotionally, and psychologically. This provides a strong foundation for friendship. Consider the following definition of a friend:

> We cannot tell the precise moment when friendship is formed. As in filling a vessel drop by drop, there is at last a drop which makes it run over; so in a series of kindness there is at last one which makes the heart run over.
>
> SAMUEL JOHNSON

> And what is a friend? Many things...A friend is someone you are comfortable with, someone whose company you prefer. A friend is someone you can count on—not only for support, but for honesty.
>
> A friend is one who believes in you...someone with

whom you can share your dreams. In fact, a real friend is a person you want to share all of life with—and the sharing doubles the fun.

When you are hurting and you can share your struggle with a friend, it eases the pain. A friend offers you safety and trust...Whatever you say will never be used against you.

A friend will laugh with you, but not at you.... A friend will pray with you...and for you. My friend is one who hears my cry of pain, who senses my struggle, who shares my lows as well as my highs.[1]

In such a friendship, nothing is hidden. This friendship is built on trust, and the relationship takes time to grow and develop. What better context for this kind of friendship to grow than in your marriage! How does your marriage measure up against this description? If you and your wife don't share this kind of friendship, take the initial step and see how she responds. If you have tried before and not been well received, ask God to guide and bless your efforts and then risk reaching out again.

When Pain Is a Roadblock

Perhaps your friendship with your wife is being blocked by some pain that you're dealing with. Perhaps you find yourself in a tunnel of chaos, unable to reach out to her as you'd like.

> There was a definite process by which one made people into friends, and it involved talking to them and listening to them for hours at a time.
>
> REBECCA WEST

If that's the case, let me encourage you to share your hurt with your wife. But first you may need to address that pain on your own. Don't deny your problem, your feelings, or your questions. Go into that tunnel and feel the pain. In *Honest to God,* Bill Hybels outlines four steps you can take to move from pain and despair to hope and genuine joy.[2]

First, refuse to deny the pain, the frustration, or the heartache you are experiencing. We are deceitful and hypocritical when we deny such feelings. We are not being real when we mindlessly chant "Praise the Lord!" in the face of life's harsh realities. Our parents are imperfect and caused us pain; miscarriages are times for grief; wayward teenagers tear apart their parents' hearts; unemployment brings feelings of fear and anxiety; and abuse results in devastation beyond description. This is only a sampling of the heartache that is in this world, and we need to face realities like these. We need to acknowledge our feelings of fear, loneliness, disappointment, and anger.

Second, honestly tell God how you feel. In the psalms, David repeatedly and very openly speaks of the confusion and pain in his heart: "Surely in vain I have kept my heart pure and washed my hands in innocence. For I have been stricken all day long" (Psalm 73:13-14). Often such authentic outpourings of frustration and anger are necessary steps on the path to wholeness and to genuine faith in God. If we don't ask these questions, we will simply go through the motions of believing in God and never find an inner confidence in His infinite power or His unconditional love. Share your feelings—the good and the bad—with your God, who is plenty big enough to deal with them and help you handle them.

Third, discuss your pain, disappointment, or heartache with someone else—hopefully your wife. Galatians 6:2 tells us to "share each other's troubles and problems, and so obey our Lord's command" (TLB). Relief, comfort, and healing come when we share our inner hurts with someone else. The burden somehow seems lighter. Once overwhelming issues suddenly become manageable when your wife shows she understands. Often sharing brings new insights or the suggestions of courses of action you haven't thought of. Almost always, sharing means less loneliness in your pain.

Fourth, don't hesitate to seek professional help if your unfinished business is weighty and emotionally debilitating. Hybels writes:

> Certainly the healing process requires divine intervention and spiritual growth. And, often, loving family and

friends can provide the human support and wisdom we need. But there are times when competent Christian counselors can provide the necessary blend of spiritual and psychological perspectives. They can help us uncover and understand significant events in our past. And they can help us resolve tensions and initiate more positive relationships with significant people in our lives.

Acknowledging your real feelings and dealing with them can free you to be the kind of friend Christ wants you to be. Without brushing away some cobwebs and first being transparent with ourselves, we'll be limited to a very superficial kind of friendship with anyone else.

Having dealt with your feelings to some degree, if you haven't shared with your wife, make an appointment to do so. Tell her where you hurt and explain that you truly want to be a friend to her, but your pain makes it hard for you right now. If the idea of talking so openly to your wife and letting yourself be so vulnerable is new to you, this undoubtedly sounds frightening. Let me assure you that meeting the challenge will result in greater honesty and intimacy in your marriage. Pray about taking this step and seek counsel. When you're ready, know that God will be with you. You are paving the way for a new source of strength for your marriage: genuine, intimate friendship with your wife.

Express Your Love

Make an unexpected date with your wife for lunch during the middle of the week—your treat.

The Rewards of Friendship

You probably don't need to be convinced, but friendship offers rich rewards. Consider the comments of these people: Upon the death of his friend A.H. Hallam, the poet Tennyson declared, "'Tis better to have loved and lost than never to have loved at all." Helen Keller once said, "With the death of every friend I love a part of me has been buried, but their contribution to my being of happiness, strength and understanding remains to sustain me in an altered world."

Have you experienced these truths about friendship? Thank God for those gifts! The value of friendship extends beyond emotional closeness and connectedness. Research has shown that lonely people live significantly shorter lives than the general population. In his book *The Friendship Factor,* Alan Loy McGinnis points out other benefits of friendship:

> In research at our clinic, my colleague and I have dis-
> covered that friendship is the springboard to every other
> love. Friendships spill over onto the other important
> relationships of life. People with no friends usually have
> diminished capacity for sustaining any kind of love. They
> tend to go through a succession of marriages, be estranged
> from various family members, and have trouble getting
> along at work. On the other hand, those who learn how
> to love their friends tend to make long and fulfilling mar-
> riages, get along well with the people at work, and enjoy
> their children.[3]

Whatever you or your wife's past experiences of friendship are, I strongly encourage you to cultivate friendship with your wife. What do you think of when you think of friendship? Someone who goes fishing, plays tennis, or goes to a baseball game with you? Shared activities are the point for men, but let me add that Christian men can take male friendships to a deeper level. You can come to a point of real honesty, transparency, and loyalty that makes friendship a source of important accountability and encouragement.

Many men in America are seemingly without friends. They simply don't have (or should that be "make"?) time for friendships.

Whether that's due to the structure of your workdays, your personalities, your priorities, or even our culture, the fact is that men without friends, if they're honest, experience a real emotional void in their lives. Also, too often competition rears its head. For various reasons, men often experience a degree of distrust and cautiousness around each other. Job titles can also interfere with cultivating a friendship until men view one another as God's creation—and even as a mission field of sorts. Whether men

> Having a friend is one of the greatest gifts you've ever had. Cherish it and invest in it.
>
> AUTHOR UNKNOWN

work in a plush office or dig ditches, they are all God's creatures, and they all have the same needs. This scriptural perspective can help you become close friends with other men.

Women have an easier time with friendships and have experienced different levels of friendship than men do. Our culture, for instance, permits women to be closer to each other than men can typically be with one another. Women can hug, cry, hold hands, and interlock their arms as they walk down the street, but men are not as free to do these things.

Since men are activity-oriented and women are relationally-oriented, how can you bridge that gap to become friends with your wife? Simply get interested in your wife's activities. That's one way you can be her friend. After all, you have to be a friend in order to have a friend.

The Art of Finding Friends

"If you want to have friends, be friendly." That's great advice as far as it goes, but sometimes the process of friend-finding could use a bit of a jump start. Here are some practical ideas for striking the friendship spark.

- *Carry a card.* Keep a small supply of business cards in your billfold and briefcase so it's easy to say, "Call me."
- *Drop a line.* If you meet someone you'd like to know

better, drop them a note or get on your computer and send a friendly e-mail.

- *Issue an invitation.* When you meet someone new and interesting, invite him to a sporting event, to have lunch with you, or to work out.

- *Take notes.* Write down important things you learn about a new acquaintance—birthday, family's names, and so on. Your friendship will grow faster if you're not always having to cover new ground.

- *Offer a welcome.* If someone new moves into your neighborhood or church, introduce yourself and offer to help.

- *Open your mind.* Your next best friend just might be someone you don't expect—older, younger, or simply different.

- *Leave room in your life for future friends.* Try scheduling some things to do alone—a daily walk, a stroll through a museum—with the idea that you might share that time later with a new friend.

- *Learn something new.* Take a class, join a study group, start a new hobby. The more you ask questions and participate in your new interest, the more potential friends you're apt to meet.

- *Nourish spiritual connections.* Keep your eyes open as you attend worship or other religious activities. If you meet someone who seems to share your spiritual interests, ask if he would consider praying with you on a regular basis.

- *Ask for help with a project.* It's not only a good way to get the job done, it's also a nice way to get to know someone better.

- *Offer someone a ride to a meeting or other gathering.* The gesture is usually appreciated, and the commute is a nice time to get to know each other better.

- *Keep a "yes" in your heart.* You never know whether the next person you meet will turn out to be a close friend.[4]

Five Ways to Deepen Your Friendship

As you cultivate a friendship with your wife, here are five points to consider.

1. *Assign top priority to your friendship.* How important are your friendships? Each of us does what we want to; nothing gets in the way of our doing what is most important to us. Do you say you don't have time for friends, but you find time to start a new project, read a book, catch your favorite TV program? If you really want to do something, you'll do it. If you really want to nurture your friendship with your wife, you'll do it. It will take time and effort because good, enduring friendships don't happen instantaneously. The time you invest in your friendship with your wife is time well spent.

One of the hindrances to spending time with your wife may be your kids. They do indeed demand time. But, as I say, "You were a husband to your wife before you were a father to your children." Your wife needs to be a priority if your marriage is to be strong and your children secure. After all, one of the best gifts you can give your children is to show them that Dad and Mom love each other.

2. *Cultivate transparency in your relationship.* As we saw at the beginning of this chapter, when we are honest with ourselves about who we are (emotionally and otherwise), we can be a better friend. Our willingness to be open about who we are encourages trust and openness on the part of the other person. So be yourself in your friendships.

Be yourself, first of all, to honor God who made you the unique person you are. Also, discover the freedom that comes with being who you are. When my daughter, Jenny, was in high school, she often stopped by her dad's office. One evening at the dinner table she said, "Dad, you're the same person at work as you are at home!" I considered that a real compliment to Bob. That's the way it should be. Besides, life is simpler that way. It's not good to wear a lot of masks—you might not remember which face is for which occasion!

3. *Dare to risk talking about your affection.* At our seminars, Bob and I pass out packages of 64 multicolored cards that say, "I love you because..." We encourage each guest to give these encouragers to their family members and others. Your wife will love receiving these notes—after you've completed the sentence, of course! Tape one to the steering wheel in her car, leave one in the bathroom, put it next to her plate at a meal. Don't hesitate to show your love. And it's great for your kids to see that you actively love your wife and aren't afraid to let people know it!

People who have used these cards tell us again and again what a good idea they are. I'll long remember the woman who put one card in her husband's sandwich. When he unwrapped his sandwich and took a big bite, he discovered the card but thought his wife had left the wrapper on the cheese. Then he realized he had received a special note from his wife. At first he thought his lunchtime buddies would make fun of him, but one of them said, "I wish my wife would send me a love note!" The wife who had written the note was glad she had risked sharing her affection—and I'm sure her husband was too. You men do want to know that we love you. And your wife wants to know you love her too!

4. *Learn the language of love.* Each of us needs to learn how to say "I love you." I'm not talking about only speaking aloud those three powerful words (although that's an important thing to do!). We need to also say "I love you" through our respect. Sometimes, for instance, as Bob is leaving on errands, he will ask if there's anything he can get for me while he's out. Or he might hear me say that I'd like a certain new book and—what do you know?—it shows up unexpectedly for no special reason.

I show Bob that I love him with an evening out, a new book, a

> It is the steady and merciless increase of occupations, the augmented speed at which we are always trying to live, the crowding of each day with more work than it can profitably hold, which has cost us, among other things, the undisturbed enjoyment of friends. Friendship takes time, and we have no time to give it.
>
> AGNES REPPLIER

new shirt, and taking out the trash for him. Whenever I choose to show my love this way, I say aloud to Bob, "Just another way to say, 'I love you!'" Little acts of kindness are powerful and effective ways to strengthen your friendship with your mate. Such acts of thoughtfulness show that you don't take your loved one for granted.

Certain rituals and traditions in our family also enable Bob and I to express our love for one another. We kiss each other goodnight and say, "May God bless your sleep." We celebrate our love on anniversaries and birthdays by giving each other small gifts. We telephone one another when we're apart, visit one of our favorite restaurants on special occasions, go out to lunch, attend the theater, and share hugs and corny jokes. All of these things—spontaneous acts as well as carefully planned events—make for a special friendship.

> Don't flatter yourself that friendship authorizes you to say disagreeable things to your intimates. The nearer you come into relation with a person, the more necessary do tact and courtesy become.
>
> OLIVER WENDELL HOLMES

One word of caution. Be sure that you are expressing your love in the language—the words *and* the actions—that *your spouse* will understand. Just because you feel loved when she gives you a tool set doesn't mean she feels loved when you do the same. Be a student of your wife. Know what best communicates *to her* the love you have. And keep your eyes open for common, everyday events that give you the chance to express your love.

A lawnmower, a power tool, a washer or dryer, or a treadmill may not be appropriate for your wife's birthday. Don't buy her a gift that you would like for yourself or that you would like her to use. Instead take mental notes when she points out something while visiting the mall: "That's a pretty nightie. Those dishes would look nice for a dinner place setting. What a nice vase for flowers. Wouldn't that be a nice restaurant to have dinner out at?" Pay attention to what she likes—then you'll score extra-credit points for getting her what she would like.

5. *Give your wife freedom.* As the apostle Paul writes so beautifully in 1 Corinthians 13:4, "Love is very patient and kind, never jealous or envious, never boastful or proud" (TLB). Love is never oppressive or possessive. Make sure your words and actions don't discourage your wife and keep her from growing and developing in her spirituality, her homemaking skills, and even her hobbies. Loosen the reins and give your wife permission to be all that God wants her to be. This means she must be given time away from you and the family to improve her interests and skills that might be different than yours. In order to encourage this freedom, sit down with your wife and discuss what price you and other members of the family will pay for that freedom. (Costs may include doing the dishes, vacuuming, etc.) It's got to be a team decision or one party will be hurt and angry and Satan will have a wonderful time breaking your relationship apart.

> People are lonely because they build walls instead of bridges.
>
> JOSEPH F. NEWTON

Another key area of freedom your wife needs is to have her own money so she can feel she doesn't have to come to you all the time asking for money. I continually get questions asked regarding this area. Working moms outside the home usually have their own funds, but the stay-at-home mom needs to have some financial independence too.

Your wife also needs to establish credit so that if anything happens to you, she will have this vital economic tool in place.

Freedom works both ways. You should also have freedom to become the man God wants you to be. Many men fear losing their freedom, and wives can easily make that fear a painful reality. But let me say that you men also need to carefully balance your relationships with the Lord, your wife, and your children, along with your job commitments and recreational activities. Be sure you take the necessary time to be the husband and father God calls you to be.

How can you set your wife free to become the person God would have her be? One key to setting her free is to accept her unconditionally.

Encourage your wife. Be willing to allow for shifts in your wife's friendship with you. As the seasons of your lives change, you'll notice variations in your relationship. The birth of a child, for instance, means new responsibilities, increased tiredness, an adjustment in the area of sexuality, and greater demands on your friendship. Your wife may feel that the child is more important to her than you are for a time. If left unchecked, friendship with your spouse will become strained. After the children leave home, it's crucial that you've maintained your friendship—that you still know each other and like each other. You don't want to become "business partners" held together loosely by your child-raising efforts.

Whatever the season of your life, know that a friendship that is tended, nurtured, and rooted in the Lord will endure. Know too that being your wife's friend will make your marriage more enjoyable.

Pillow Talk

- If you know you did something wrong in your relationship, how quickly would you apologize?

- Describe an exciting evening date.

- Name a love song that best describes your feelings for me.

- Where do you picture our relationship ten years from now?

Love Gestures

- I love a man who gives priority to me and the family (after God).

- I love a man who never criticizes me in front of others.

- I love a man who notices my new dress and new hairdo.

- I love a man who is involved with his children's activities.

- I love a man who calls me during the day just to see how I'm doing.
- I love a man who tells me what a good cook I am.
- I love a man who tells the children what a good person I am.
- I love a man who takes pride in how he dresses.
- I love a man who has a good sense of humor.

14

Do You Love Me?

Let love be without hypocrisy...
cling to what is good.

ROMANS 12:9

The greatest question a wife ever asks is, "Do you love me?" You men are likely to respond, "I told you I loved you at the altar, and nothing has changed." This certainly points out how differently the sexes perceive "Do you love me?" Gentlemen, you can tell your wife you love her every morning, and at the day's end, she will ask, "Do you love me?" Oh, it might not always be a verbal question, but in her mind she wonders. This doesn't mean it's futile to keep telling her! The amount of assurance a wife needs depends on her, but all wives need to hear their husbands say, "I love you."

One of the greatest needs that a wife has is to feel secure, to know her man loves her. When men hear that women seek security, they tend to think in terms of financial security—a new car, a big house, a good job. Yes, women think that way, too, but finances aren't nearly as important as having strong *emotional* security—feeling that she is loved and that you will always be there when she needs your strong arms to hug her tightly and you to whisper in her ear, "I love you!"

Unlocking the secret of how to give your mate this emotional security is a lot easier than satisfying her secondary need of financial security. Men tend to think that because they perceive that marriage and family is going well, so do their wives. Wrong. Most men will rate their marriages higher than their wives do. One of my friends told her husband, "You need to get with the program," and he asked, "What program?" Part of that program is letting your wife know she is loved. Bob must know I need that assurance because every day he will tell me, "Just another way to say that I love you!" when he does something for me. He's a wise husband because he knows that I recognize an act of kindness as an expression of his love to me and his verbal reminder really reassures me.

> Love never hides in the shadows or in darkness...It grows with trust, honesty, and compassion.
>
> AUTHOR UNKNOWN

When you said "I do" at the altar, you meant that the deal is closed and you are in the marriage relationship until "death do you part." Yes, you still need occasional reassurance that you're loved and appreciated, but your wife, who also said "I do," needs continued assurance that you still love her. When she continues to ask if you love her, what she is really checking is, "Is our relationship okay?"

As men you may have a difficult time realizing why this is such a big deal to her. Remember, I said earlier in this book, "Men are weird and women are strange." This is an area where women are certainly strange. However, if you learn the secret of saying "I love you" in ways that reach your wife's heart, the reward will be great...and beyond your imagination.

There are certain signals that will tell you your wife needs support and reassurance. Things seem to be going smoothly and all of a sudden—boom! out of nowhere comes odd behavior:

1. *Arguments*—From nowhere or for seemingly nothing, your wife presents some sort of conflict. You ask, "Where did that come from?" After all you thought everything was going just fine.

2. *Escape*—You're upset or just want time alone. This is normal for males, but when you do this, your wife will think there's something wrong or that you don't love her anymore.

3. *Stops communicating*—When silence occurs in a relationship, your wife will jump from A to Z and think, "It must be my fault. He doesn't love me anymore."

4. *Stops feeling important*—When your self-worth takes a nose dive, you turn from being positive to feeling negative. When your wife all of a sudden turns negative, this is a red flag that she needs encouraged and listened to.

5. *When your job takes you away from home*—Even though you might have to do what you have to do to provide financial security, your wife might read into this awayness that you don't want to be at home with her. It is very important to give extra attention to your wife when you have to be away.

6. *Old issues reappearing*—Your mate keeps bringing up things from the past. Just because you think a certain topic has been talked out, that doesn't mean she feels the same way. When this recycling of issues appears, check to see if your wife's emotional security is feeling threatened. Then reassure her!

So What Do I Do?

Now that you know that emotional insecurity is a big deal in your wife's life, what can you do? My word of wisdom is to let your wife know continually that she is loved. It doesn't always have to be a big deal either. A simple "I love you," an act of kindness, a box of candy, an occasional bouquet of flowers, an evening out (just the two of you), a two- or three-day getaway. Last year Bob and I made a pledge that we would hug each other at least once a day. We've often had to remind each other of this agreement, but it has had a positive impact on our relationship.

Hold your wife's face, look into her eyes, and express with great passion, "I truly love you, and I will be here to comfort you, protect you, and enjoy our friendship forever." She'll love this!

> If I speak with the tongues of men and of angels, but do not have love, I have become a noisy gong or a clanging cymbal. If I have the gift of prophecy, and know all mysteries and all knowledge; and if I have all faith, so as to remove mountains, but do not have love, I am nothing.
>
> 1 Corinthians 13:1-2

Yes, it's a lot easier to do these things when everything is rosy with your relationship. How about when things aren't so hot? The principle is the same. You might need space to cool off, but when you come back together there must be resolution and assurance given. Bob and I make it a point to resolve any conflicts before we go to sleep at night. This has worked very well for us. Often we have not gotten very much sleep, but we talk and listen, talk and listen.

We had some very dear friends who were having difficulty in their marriage. Bob took the husband aside and I took the wife aside, and we encouraged them to start dating again, just as they did when they first met. After about six months of him chasing her and her getting caught, they recaptured the emotional feel of love. Sometimes it is wise to repeat those things you did when you first met. The flowers, the walks on the beach, the picnics, the kissing on the lonely road of town. Let your wife know she is very desirable.

Pillow Talk

- What are your goals for life?
- Was there a point in your life when you had a "spiritual awakening"? Share what it meant to you.
- Name your favorite book and what inspiration you received from it.
- If you had to eat the same food for a week, what food would you choose?
- What period of history would you most like to live in?

Love Gestures

- I love a man who gives me freedom to grow.
- I love a man who loves my smile.
- I love a man who enjoys being with me.
- I love a man who comes home on time.
- I love a man who is interested in my day.
- I love a man who doesn't tell off-color jokes.
- I love a man who wants to be the spiritual leader of our home.
- I love a man who uses good manners when we are out for the evening.
- I love a man who knows how to manage our finances well.

I Need You

I need you in my times of strength and in my weakness;

I need you when you hurt as much as when I hurt.

There is no longer the choice as to what we will share.

We will either share all of life or be fractured persons.

I didn't marry you out of need or to be needed.

We were not driven by instincts or emptiness;

We made a choice to love.

But I think something supernatural happens at the point of marriage commitment (or maybe it's actually natural).

A husband comes into existence; a wife is born.

He is a whole man before and after, but at a point in time he becomes a man who also is a husband.

That is—a man who needs a wife.

She is a whole woman before and after.

But from now on she needs him.

She is herself but now also part of a new unit.

Maybe this is what is meant in saying, "What God hath joined together."

Could it be He really does something special at "I do"?

Your despair is mine even if you don't tell me about it.

But when you do tell, the sharing is easier for me;

And you also can then share from my strength in that weakness.[1]

15

A Love Song

Above all, love each other deeply.

1 PETER 4:8

A dynamic book in the Bible gives us the pattern of married love as God intended it to be. The Song of Solomon's revelation is in such detail that it can serve as a guide and model for your marriage. The Song of Solomon, also known as the Song of Songs, is a story about the marriage between the king of Israel and a very lovely, naïve, country girl whom he met in the vineyards of his kingdom. This true-to-life episode dealing with real-life situations was written down through the inspiration of the Holy Spirit. Three thousand years later we still read it and sense that marriages truly please and honor God.

You may be surprised to find such vivid expressions of love in the Bible. You'll also be amazed at the broad range of practical insights to be gleaned from this book of Scripture. Biblical principles transcend time and cultural differences; Song of Solomon captures beautifully the poetry of love between a man and a woman.

Historians over the years have disagreed about what Song of Solomon is teaching. Some argue that it talks about love and marriage; others believe it is referring to Jesus Christ and His love for us. I believe both arguments are valid since Christian marriage is a reflection of Christ's love for His church. Ephesians 5:25 says, "Husbands, love your wives, just as Christ also loved the church and gave Himself up for her." (By the way, the woman is referred to as "Shulamith." Whether this is her name or her nationality is unclear...and doesn't matter. We can learn a lot from this relationship.)

God's design for purity in love and marriage has always been at odds with the world's ideas. Whereas Scripture portrays marriage as a model representing Jesus Christ's relationship with the church, the world looks upon sex as a means of pleasure. People indulge in sex, but they don't comprehend the idea of holiness and purity in the sexual relationship. Solomon teaches us the truth that romantic love is God's gift to us in marriage.

In Song of Solomon we find a vineyard maiden tanned by the hot sun of the fields being courted by the king of Israel. She felt inferior to the light-skinned maidens of Solomon's court, and she thought she was unworthy to be Solomon's queen. But Solomon, in all his wisdom, built up her self-image. He praised her every opportunity he could. He lifted her up; he voiced appreciation of her physical appearance; he compared her with all the other women and found none other more attractive and inviting. She was flawless and perfect in his eyes. He not only did this in courtship, but throughout their marriage. Note this principle of giving praise to our mates: Both husbands and wives need to hear praise!

Express Your Love

What about your mate sparks your
romantic interest? Let her know!

Not only did Solomon praise his wife, he also didn't criticize her. One of Bob's and my favorite verses is found in Ephesians 4:29, which reads, "Do not let any unwholesome talk come out of your mouths, but only what is helpful for building others up according to their needs, that it may benefit those who listen" (NIV). Never in this book does Solomon utter one word of criticism. His words are always positive and uplifting. This consideration bore much fruit and blessings in their marriage. By his praise, Solomon let everyone know that he loved his wife more than anything in the whole kingdom. As Solomon treated her as a queen, she became just that. Isn't it amazing how we become how we are treated and respected?

In the following paraphrase by S. Craig Glickman, the love and affection found in the Song of Solomon is clearly developed. Notice how this couple built their love for each other in both physical and emotional ways. Share this interpretative paraphrase with your wife. You'll discover how the love between a husband and wife is blessed by God and is a form of worship to Him.

May God richly bless you as you read this interpretation of the Song of Solomon.[1]

The Most Beautiful Love Song Ever Written
Song of Solomon

SHULAMITH'S FIRST DAYS IN THE PALACE (1:2-11)

The King's fiancée, Shulamith, in soliloquy: How I wish he would shower me with kisses, for his exquisite kisses are more desirable than the finest wine. The gentle fragrance of your cologne brings the enchantment of springtime. Yes, it is the rich fragrance of your heart that awakens my love and respect. Yes, it is your character that brings you admiration from every girl of the court. How I long for you to come take me with you to run and laugh through the countryside of this kingdom. (You see, the King had brought me to the kingdom's palace.)

Women of the court to the King: We will always be very thankful and happy because of you, O King. For we love to speak of the inspiring beauty of your love.

Shulamith in soliloquy: They rightly love a person like you, my King.

Shulamith to women of the court: I realize that I do not display the fair and delicate skin of one raised in the comfort of a palace. I am darkened from the sun—indeed, as dark as the tents of the humble nomads I used to work beside. But now I might say that I am also as dark as the luxurious drapery of the King's palace. Nevertheless, what loveliness I do have is not so weak that the gaze of the sun should make it bow its head in shame. And if the glare of the sun could not shame me, please know that neither will the glare of your contempt. I could not help it that my step-brothers were angry with me and demanded that I work in the vineyard they had leased from the King. It was possible for me to care for it and for the vineyard of my own appearance.

Shulamith to King: Please tell me, whom I love so deeply, where you take your royal flock for its afternoon rest. I don't want to search randomly for you, wandering about like a woman of the streets.

Women of the court to Shulamith: If you do not know, O fairest among women, why not simply go ahead and follow the trail of the flocks, and then pasture your flock beside the shepherd's huts?

King to Shulamith: Your presence captivates attention as thoroughly as a single mare among a hundred stallions. And how perfectly your lovely jewelry and necklace adorn your lovely face.

Women of the court to Shulamith: We shall make even more elegant necklaces of gold and silver to adorn her face.

IN A PALACE ROOM (1:12-14)

Shulamith in soliloquy: While my King was dining at his table, my perfume refreshed me with its soothing fragrance. For my King is the fragrance and my thoughts of him are like a sachet of perfume hung around my neck, over my heart, continually refreshing me. How dear he is to me, as dear as the delicate henna blossoms in the oasis of En-Gedi. What joy I have found in that oasis!

IN THE COUNTRYSIDE (1:15–2:7)

King to Shulamith: You are so beautiful, my love. You are so beautiful. Your soft eyes are as gentle as doves.

Shulamith to King: And you are handsome, my love, and so enjoyable. It's so wonderful to walk through our home of nature together. Here the cool grass is a soft couch to lie upon, to catch our breath and to gaze at the beams and rafters of our house— the towering cedars and cypresses all around. Lying here I feel like a rose from the valley of Sharon, the loveliest flower in the valley.

King to Shulamith: Only the loveliest flower in the valley? No, my love. To me you are like a flower among thorns compared with any other woman in the world.

Shulamith to King: And you, my precious King, are like a fruitful apple tree among the barren trees of the forest compared with all the men in the world.

Shulamith in soliloquy: No longer do I labor in the heat of the sun. I find cool rest in the shade of this apple tree. Nourishment from its magical fruit brings me the radiant health only love brings. And he loves me so much. Even when he brings me to the great royal banquets attended by the most influential people in this kingdom and beyond, he is never so concerned for them that his love and his care for me is not as plain as a royal banner lifted high above my head. How dear he is to me! My delightful peace in his love makes me so weak from joy that I must rest in his arms for strength. Yet such loving comfort makes me more joyful and weaker still. How I wish he could lay me down beside him and embrace me! But how important it is I promise, with the gentle gazelle and deer of the countryside as my witnesses, not to attempt to awaken love until love is pleased to awaken itself.

ON THE WAY TO THE COUNTRYSIDE (2:8-17)

Shulamith in soliloquy: I hear my beloved. Look! He is coming to visit. And he is as dashing as a young stag leaping upon the mountains, springing upon the hills. There he is, standing at the door, trying to peer through the window and peep through the lattice. At last he speaks.

King to Shulamith: Come, my darling, my fair one, come with me. For look, the winter has passed. The rain is over and gone. The blossoms have appeared in the land. The time of singing has come, and the voice of the turtledove has been heard in the land. The fig tree has ripened its figs, and the vines in blossom have given forth fragrance. Let us go, my darling, my lovely one; come along with me. O my precious, gentle dove. You have been like a dove in the clefts of the mountain rocks, in the hidden places along the mountain trails. Now come out from the hidden place and let me see you. Let me hear the coo of your voice. For your voice is sweet and you are as gracefully beautiful as a dove in flight silhouetted against a soft blue sky. My love, what we have together is a valuable treasure; it is like a garden of the loveliest flowers in the world. Let us promise each other to catch any foxes that could spoil our garden when now at long last it blossoms for us.

Shulamith in soliloquy: My beloved belongs to me and I belong to him—this tender King who grazes his flock among the lilies.

Shulamith to the King: How I long for the time when all through the night, until the day takes its first breath and the morning shadows flee from the sun, that you, my beloved King, might be a gazelle upon the hills of my breasts.

SHULAMITH WAITS FOR HER FIANCÉ (3:1-5)

Shulamith in soliloquy: How I miss the one I love so deeply. I could not wait to see him. I thought to myself, "I must get up and find him. I will get up now and look around the streets and squares of the city for him. Surely I'll be able to find this one I love so much." But I could not find him. When the night watchmen of the city found me, I immediately asked them if they had seen this one I loved so deeply. But they had not. Yet no sooner did I pass from them than I found my beloved. I held on and on and would not let him go until I could bring him to my home. I still held on until my fearful anxiety left me and I felt peaceful once again. How hard it is to be patient! You women of the court, we must promise ourselves, by the gazelles and deer of the field, not to awaken love until love is pleased to awaken itself.

THE WEDDING DAY (3:6-11)

Poet: What can this be coming from the outskirts of the city like columns of smoke, perfumed clouds of myrrh and frankincense, clouds of the scented powders of the merchant? Look! It is the royal procession with Solomon carried upon his lavish couch by his strongest servants. And take a look at all those soldiers around it! That is the imperial guard, the sixty mightiest warriors in the entire kingdom. Each one is an expert with his weapon and valiant in battle. Yet now each one has a sword at his side only for the protection of the King and his bride. Look at the luxurious couch Solomon is carried on. He has had it made especially for this day. He made its frame from the best timber of Lebanon. Its posts are made of silver, its back of gold, and its seat of royal purple cloth. And do you see its delicate craftsmanship! It reflects the skill of the women of the court who gave their best work out of love for the King and his bride. Let us all go out and look upon King Solomon wearing his elegant wedding crown. Let us go out and see him on the most joyful day of his life.

THE WEDDING NIGHT (4:1–5:1)

King to Shulamith: You are so beautiful my love, you are so beautiful. Your soft eyes are as gentle as doves from behind your wedding veil. Your hair is as captivating as the flowing movement of a flock descending a mountain at sunset. Your full and lovely smile is as cheerful and sparkling as pairs of young lambs scurrying up from a washing. And only a thread of scarlet could have outlined your lips so perfectly. Your cheeks flush with the redness of the pomegranate's hue. Yet you walk with dignity and stand with the strength of a fortress. Your necklace sparkles like the shields upon the fortress tower. But your breasts are as soft and gentle as fawns grazing among lilies. And now at last, all through the night—until the day takes its first breath and the morning shadows flee from the sun—I will be a gazelle upon the hills of your perfumed breasts. You are completely and perfectly beautiful, my love, and flawless in every way. Now bring your thoughts completely to me, my love. Leave your fears in the far away mountains and rest in the security of my arms. You excite me, my darling bride; you excite me with but a glance of your eyes, with but a strand of your necklace. How wonderful are your caresses, my beloved bride. Your love is more sweetly intoxicating than the finest wine. And the fragrance of your perfume is better than the finest spices. The richness of honey and milk is under your tongue, my love. And the fragrance of your garments is like the fragrance of the forests of Lebanon. You are a beautiful garden fashioned only for me, my darling bride. Yes, like a garden kept only for me. Or like a fresh fountain sealed just for me. Your garden is overflowing with beautiful and delicate flowers of every scent and color. It is a paradise of pomegranates with luscious fruit, with henna blossoms and nard, nard and saffron, calamus and cinnamon with trees of frankincense, myrrh and aloes with all the choicest of spices. And you are pure as fresh water, yet more than a mere fountain. You are a spring for many gardens—a well of life-giving water. No, even more, you are like the fresh streams flowing from Lebanon which give life to the entire countryside.

Shulamith to King: Awake, O north wind, and come, wind of the south. Let your breezes blow upon my garden and carry its fragrant spices to my beloved. May he follow the enchanting spices to my garden and come in to enjoy its luscious fruit.

King to Shulamith: I have rejoiced in the richness of your garden, my darling bride. I have been intoxicated by the fragrance of your myrrh and perfume. I have tasted the sweetness of your love like honey. I have enjoyed the sweetness of your love like an exquisite wine and the refreshment of your love like the coolness of milk.

Poet to couple: Rejoice in your lovemaking as you would rejoice at a great feast, O lovers. Eat and drink from this feast to the fullest. Drink, drink and be drunk with one another's love.

Shulamith in soliloquy: I was half asleep when I heard the sound of my beloved husband knocking gently upon the door of our palace chamber. He whispered softly, "I'm back from the countryside, my love, my darling, my perfect wife." My only answer was a mumbled, "I've already gone to sleep, my dear." After all, I had already prepared for bed. I had washed my face and put on my old nightgown. But then my beloved gently opened the door and I realized I really wanted to see him. I had hesitated too long though. By the time I arose to open the door, he had already walked away, leaving only a gift of my favorite perfume as a reminder of his love for me. Deep within my heart I was reawakened to my love for him. It was just that the fatigue and distractions of the day had brought my hesitating response. I decided to try to find him. I threw on my clothes, went outside the palace and began to call out to him. But things went from bad to worse. The night watchmen of the city mistook me for a secretive criminal sneaking about in the night. They arrested me in their customarily rough style, then jerking my shawl from my head they saw the face of their newly found suspect—a "great" police force we have! O, you women of the court, if you see my beloved King, please tell him that I deeply love him, that I am lovesick for him.

Women of the court to Shulamith: What makes your husband better than any other, O fairest of women? What makes him so great that you request so fervently of us?

Shulamith to women of the court: My beloved husband is strikingly handsome, the first to be noticed among ten thousand men. When I look at him, I see a face with a tan more richly golden than gold itself. His hair is as black as a raven's feathers and as lovely as palm leaves atop the stately palm tree. When I look into his eyes, they are as gentle as doves peacefully resting by streams of water. They are as pure and clear as health can make them. When he places his cheek next to mine, it is as fragrant as a garden of perfumed flowers. His soft lips are as sweet and scented as lilies dripping with nectar. And how tender are his fingers like golden velvet when he touches me! He is a picture of strength and vitality. His stomach is as firm as a plate of ivory rippling with sapphires. And his legs are as strong and elegant as alabaster pillars set upon pedestals of fine gold. His appearance is like majestic Mt. Lebanon, prominent with its towering cedars. But beyond this, the words of his heart are full of charm and delight. He is completely wonderful in every way. This is the one I love so deeply, and this is the one who is my closest friend, O women of the palace court.

Women of the court to Shulamith: Where has your beloved gone, then, O fairest among women? Where has he gone? We will help you find him.

Shulamith to women of the court: Oh, I know him well enough to know where he has gone. He likes to contemplate as he walks through the garden and cares for his special little flock among the lilies. I know him, for I belong to him and he belongs to me—this gentle shepherd who pastures his flock among the lilies.

THE PROBLEM RESOLVED *(6:4-13)*

King to Shulamith: My darling, did you know that you are as lovely as the city of Tirzah glittering on the horizon of night? No, more than that you are as lovely as the fair city of Jerusalem. Your beauty is as breathtaking as scores of marching warriors. (No, do not look at me like that now, my love; I have more to tell you.) Do you remember what I said on our wedding night? It is still just as true. Your hair is as captivating as the flowing movement of a flock descending a mountain at sunset. Your lovely smile is as cheerful and sparkling as pairs of young lambs scurrying up from a washing. And your cheeks still flush with the redness of the pomegranate's hue.

King in soliloquy: The palace is full of its aristocratic ladies and dazzling mistresses belonging to the noblemen of the court. But my lovely wife, my dove, my flawless one, is unique among them all. And these ladies and mistresses realize it too. They too must praise her. As we approached them in my chariot, they eventually perceived that we were together again.

Women of the court to one another: Who is that on the horizon like the dawn, now fair as the moon but now plain and bright as the sun and as majestic as scores of marching warriors?

Shulamith in the chariot in soliloquy: I went down to the garden where I knew my King would be. I wanted to see if the fresh flowers and fruits of spring had come. I wanted to see if our reunion might bring a new season of spring love for my husband and me. Before I knew what happened, we were together again and riding past the palace court in his chariot. I can still hear them calling out, "Return, return O Shulamith; return that we may gaze at the beloved wife of the King."

King to Shulamith: How they love to look upon the incomparable grace and beauty of a queen.

IN THE ROYAL BEDROOM (7:1-10)

King to Shulamith: How delicate are your feet in sandals, my royal prince's daughter! The curves of your hips are as smooth and graceful as the curves of elegant jewelry, perfectly fashioned by the skillful hands of a master artist. As delectable as a feast of wine and bread is your stomach—your navel is like the goblet of wine and your stomach is the soft warm bread. Your breasts are as soft and gentle as fawns grazing among the lilies, twins of a gazelle, and your neck is smooth as ivory to the touch. Your eyes are as peaceful as the pools of water in the valley of Heshbon, near the gates of the populous city. Yet how strong you walk in wisdom and discretion. You are indeed as majestically beautiful as Mt. Carmel. Your long glowing hair is as cool and soft as silken threads draped round my neck, yet strong enough to bind me as your captive forever. How lovely and delightful you are, my dear, and how especially delightful is your love! You are as graceful and splendorous as a palm tree silhouetted against the sky. Yes, a palm tree—and your breasts are its luscious fruit.

I think I shall climb my precious palm tree and take its tender fruit gently into my hand. O my precious one, let your breasts be like the tender fruit to my taste, and now let me kiss you and breathe your fragrant breath. Let me kiss you and taste a sweetness better than wine.

Shulamith to King: And savor every drop, my lover, and let its sweetness linger long upon your lips, and let every drop of this wine bring a peaceful sleep.

Shulamith in soliloquy: I belong to my beloved husband and he loves me from the depths of his soul.

IN THE COUNTRYSIDE (7:11–8:14)

Shulamith to King: Spring's magic flowers have perfumed the pastel countryside and enchanted the hearts of all lovers. Come, my precious lover; every delicious fruit of spring is ours for the taking. Let us return to our springtime cottage of towering cedars and cypresses where the plush green grass is its endless carpet and the orchids are its shelves for every luscious fruit. I have prepared a basketful for you, my love, to give you in a sumptuous banquet of love beneath the sky. I wish we could pretend you were my brother, my real little brother. I could take you outside to play, and playfully kiss you whenever I wished. But then I could also take your hand and bring you inside and you could teach me and share with me your deep understanding of life. Then how I wish you would lay me down beside you and love me.

Shulamith to women of the court: I encourage you not to try to awaken love until love is pleased to awaken itself. How wonderful it is when it blossoms in the proper season.

Shulamith to King: Do you remember where our love began? Under the legendary sweetheart tree, of course, where every love begins and grows and then brings forth a newborn child, yet not without the pain of birth. Neither did our love begin without the pain, the fruitful pain of birth. O, my darling lover, make me your most precious possession held securely in your arms, held close to your heart. True love is as strong and irreversible as the onward march of death. True love never ceases to care, and it would no more give up the beloved than the grave would give up the dead. The fires of true love can never be quenched because the source of its flame is God himself. Even were a river of rushing water to pass over it, the flame would yet shine forth. Of all the gifts in the world, this priceless love is the most precious and possessed only by those to whom it is freely given. For no man could purchase it with money, even the richest man in the world.

King to Shulamith: Do you remember how it was given to us?

Shulamith to King: My love, I truly believe I was being prepared for it long before I even dreamed of romance. I remember hearing my brothers talking one evening. It was shortly after my father died, and they were concerned to raise me properly, to prepare me for the distant day of marriage. They were like a roomful of fathers debating about what to do with their only daughter. They finally resolved simply to punish and restrict me if I were promiscuous but to reward and encourage me if I were chaste. How thankful I am that I made it easy for them. I could see even when I was very young that I wanted to keep myself for the one dearest man in my life. And then you came. And everything I ever wanted I found in you. There I was, working daily in the vineyard my brothers had leased from you. And you "happened" to pass by and see me. That's how our love began. I remember when I worked in that vineyard that a thousand dollars went to you and two hundred dollars for the ones taking care of its fruit for you. Now I am your vineyard, my lover, and I gladly give the entire thousand dollars of my worth to you; I give myself completely, withholding nothing of my trust, my thoughts, my care, my love. But my dear King, let us not forget that two hundred dollars belongs to the ones who took care of the fruit of my vineyard for you. How thankful we must be to my family who helped prepare me for you.

King to Shulamith: My darling, whose home is the fragrant garden, everyone listens for the sound of your voice, but let me alone hear it now.

Shulamith to King: Hurry, then, my beloved. And again be like a gazelle or young stag on the hills of my perfumed breasts.

Pillow Talk

- What is your favorite season of the year? Why?
- Describe the time you were most proud of your mate.
- How many broken bones have you had?
- Describe your worst fear as a child.
- Where do you believe you go when you die?[2]

Love Gestures

- I love a man who says "I need you."
- I love a man who has good manners.
- I love a man who will cuddle with me on the couch.
- I love a man who gets along with my family.

The storm was raging. The sea was beating against
the rocks in huge, chasing waves. The lightning was
flashing, the thunder was roaring, the wind was
blowing; but the little bird was sound asleep in the
crevice of the rock, its head tucked serenely under its wing.
That is peace: to be able to sleep in the storm!
In Christ we are relaxed and at peace in the midst
of the confusions, bewilderments and perplexities
of this life. The storm rages, but our hearts are at rest.
We have found peace—at last!

BILLY GRAHAM

16

Love Is for a Lifetime

Love is not only something you
feel. It's something you do.

David Wilkerson

One of the great love stories of my life is how my Bob has been my caregiver for the last ten years. From my first being diagnosed with life-threatening M.A.L.T. cell lymphoma, a form of low-grade non-Hodgkin's leukemia, in 1997 until today, he has stepped up to the plate and honored his "I do" from our wedding some 51 years ago. Little did we realize when we were so young that our promise "until death do us part" would be tested.

Bob has loved me during the good days of our life together, and he continues to love me during the "valley of death" days. He has been right beside me as we've gone through this journey through cancer. He has stood beside me at the height of my glamor years, and he has loved me when he has walked into the hospital room and viewed me with all kinds of medical devices attached to my frail body, an oxygen mask around my nose and mouth, a Hickman catheter inserted in my chest to assist in getting valuable liquids into my body, a drainage tube, and an IV giving me hydration. There were all kinds of beeps and noises coming from all the fancy instruments.

Bob has transported me to endless doctor's appointments, waiting patiently for endless hours while I've been examined and given chemotherapy and radiation treatments. He has visited me for hours while I lay in bed in the hospital.

This kind of love is for a lifetime. It's beyond description. It is the love that every wife wants from her husband. Without a doubt I am a wife who knows she is loved.

Yes, love is for a lifetime. My heart is thrilled when I see older couples walking down the beach holding hands. I realize that here is a couple who meant what they said at the altar of their marriage:

> For better or worse,
>
> in sickness and in health,
>
> for richer or poorer,
>
> until death do us part.

Notes

Introduction

1. These *Love Gestures* are statements women have shared when asked, "What makes a woman feel loved?"

Chapter 4—Beyond the Wedding

1. Larry Crabb, *The Marriage Builder* (Grand Rapids, MI: Zondervan, 1982), p. 22.

2. Denis Waitley, *Seeds of Greatness* (New York: Pocket Books, Division of Simon & Schuster, Inc., 1983), p. 160.

Chapter 5—Concentrate on the Positive

1. Larry Crabb, *The Marriage Builder* (Grand Rapids, MI: Zondervan, 1982), pp. 105-06.

2. Dennis and Barbara Rainey, *Building Your Mate's Self-Esteem* (San Bernardino, CA: Here's Life Publishers, 1986), pp. 34-35.

3. Bill Hybels, *Honest to God* (Grand Rapids, MI: Zondervan, 1990), pp. 53-54.

Chapter 6—Go to the Instruction Manual

1. H. Norman Wright, *Quiet Times for Couples* (Eugene, OR: Harvest House Publishers, 1990), p. 35.

Chapter 7—Be Willing to Walk Your Talk

1. Robert Fulghum, *All I Really Need to Know I Learned in Kindergarten* (New York: Ballantine Books, 1986), pp. 29-31.

2. Ibid., p. 31.

3. H. Norman Wright, *Making Peace with Your Partner* (Waco, TX: Word Books, 1988), adapted from pp. 173-74.

4. Quoted in Mordecai L. Brill, Marlene Halpin, and William H. Genne, eds., *Writing Your Own Wedding* (Chicago: Follett, 1979), p. 88.

Chapter 8—Women Love to Be Loved

1. Patrick M. Morley, *The Man in the Mirror* (Brentwood, TN: Wolgemuth & Hyatt Publishers, Inc., 1989), p. 100.

2. Florence Littauer, Marita Littauer, and Lauren Littauer Briggs, *Making the Blue Plate Special* (Colorado Springs: Life Journey-Cook Communications Ministries, 2006), pp. 205-06.

3. Dennis and Barbara Rainey, *Building Your Mate's Self-Esteem* (San Bernardino, CA: Here's Life Publishers, 1986), p. 67, adapted.

Chapter 9—Knowing and Meeting Your Wife's Needs

1. Willard F. Harley, Jr., *His Needs, Her Needs* (Tarrytown, NJ: Fleming H. Revell, 1986), p. 10.

2. Kevin Leman, *Sex Begins in the Kitchen* (Ventura, CA: Regal Books, 1981).

3. Dwight Small, *After You've Said I Do* (Tarrytown, NJ: Fleming H. Revell, 1968) p. 244.

4. H. Norman Wright, *Communication: Key to Your Marriage* (Ventura, CA: Regal Books, 1974), p. 52.

5. John Powell, *Why Am I Afraid to Tell You Who I Am?* (Niles, IL: Argus Communications, 1969), adapted from pp. 54-62.

6. Florence Littauer, *After Every Wedding Comes a Marriage* (Eugene, OR: Harvest House, 1981), adapted from pp. 168-76.

7. Wright, *Communication,* adapted from pp. 71-77.

Chapter 10—The Continuing Needs of a Wife

1. Emilie Barnes, *Meet Me Where I Am, Lord* (Eugene, OR: Harvest House Publishers, 2006), adapted from pp. 125-26.

Chapter 11—Becoming One, Though Different

1. Dr. Charles C. Ryrie, *The Ryrie Study Bible, New American Standard Translation* (Chicago: Moody Press, 1978), p. 1478.

2. Joyce Brothers, *What Every Woman Should Know About Men* (New York: Ballantine Books, 1981), p. 31.

3. Doreen Kimura, "Male Brain, Female Brain: The Hidden Differences," *Psychology Today,* November 1985, p. 56.

4. William and Nancy Carmichael with Dr. Timothy Boyd, *That Man! Understanding the Difference Between You and Your Husband* (Nashville: Thomas Nelson, 1980), adapted from chapter 2.

5. Dr. Daniel G. Amen, M.D., *Healing the Hardware of the Soul* (New York: The Free Press, 2002), p. 66.

6. Adapted from Warren Farrell, *Why Men Are the Way They Are* (New York: McGraw-Hill, 1986), p. 139.

7. Carol Gilligan, *In a Different World* (Cambridge, MA: Howard University Press, 1981), p. 8.

8. T.B. Hoffer, et al., www.physicstoday.org/vol-59/iss-6/pdf/p44table1.pdf, 2004.

9. James Campbell, Jr., "An Idea Whose Time Has Past," Master's thesis, University of Wisconsin Graduate School, Education, 2003.

10. Shilpa Banerji, "Women Professors Lag in Tenured Salary," www.diverseducation.com/artman/publish/article_6571.shtml, Oct. 2006.

11. Mary Conroy, "Sexism in Our Schools: Training Girls for Failure," *Better Homes and Gardens,* February 1988, pp. 44-48.

12. Carmichael, Carmichael, and Boyd, *That Man!,* adapted from chapter 4.

13. For information on Littauer books check out the bookstore at CLASServices, www.classservices.com or Amazon.com.

14. Quoted in Harold J. Sala, *Today Can Be Different* (Ventura, CA: Regal Books, 1988), part of the devotion for July 6.

Chapter 12—The Impact of Temperaments

1. Florence Littauer, *After Every Wedding Comes a Marriage* (Eugene, OR: Harvest House Publishers, 1981), p. 22.

2. For permission to make copies and for more information on temperaments, including videos, books, test sheets, etc., contact CLASS, P.O. Box 66810, Albuquerque, NM 87193, (505) 899-4283, www.classservices.com.

3. Permission granted by Florence Littauer and CLASS to use this material on temperaments.

Chapter 13—Being a Friend with Your Partner

1. Louis and Colleen Evans, Jr., *My Lover, My Friend* (Old Tappan, NJ: Fleming H. Revell, 1976), pp. 121-22.

2. Bill Hybels, *Honest to God* (Grand Rapids, MI: Zondervan, 1990), pp. 101-04.

3. Alan Loy McGinnis, *The Friendship Factor* (Minneapolis: Augsburg, 1979), p. 9.

4. Emilie Barnes, *The Twelve Teas of Friendship* (Eugene, OR: Harvest House Publishers, 2001), pp. 12-13, adapted.

Chapter 14—Do You Love Me?

1. Jerry and Barbara Cook, *Choosing to Love* (Ventura, CA: Regal Books, 1982), pp. 78-80.

Chapter 15—A Love Song

1. Taken from S. Craig Glickman, *A Song for Lovers,* ©1976 by InterVarsity Christian Fellowship of the USA. Used by permission of S. Craig Glickman.

2. These *Pillow Talk* questions came from Mom's Family Preserves, "Sweet Talk to Couples," created by Pam Phillips and Sue Winans.

Harvest House Books
by Bob & Emilie Barnes

Bob & Emilie Barnes

*15-Minute Devotions
for Couples*

*A Little Book of Manners
for Boys*

*Minute Meditations
for Couples*

Bob Barnes

*15 Minutes Alone
with God for Men*

*500 Handy Hints for
Every Husband*

Men Under Construction

Minute Meditations for Men

*What Makes a Man
Feel Loved*

Emilie Barnes

The 15-Minute Organizer

15 Minutes Alone with God

*15 Minutes of Peace
with God*

*15 Minutes with God
for Grandma*

*500 Time-Saving Hints
for Women*

Be My Refuge

Cleaning Up the Clutter

*Emilie's Creative
Home Organizer*

*Everything I Know
I Learned in My Garden*

*Everything I Know
I Learned over Tea*

Friendship Teas to Go

*A Grandma
Is a Gift from God*

Home Warming

If Teacups Could Talk

I Need Your Strength, Lord

An Invitation to Tea

Join Me for Tea

*Keep It Simple
for Busy Women*

Let's Have a Tea Party!

A Little Book of Manners

Meet Me Where I Am, Lord

*Minute Meditations
for Busy Moms*

*Minute Meditations for Healing
and Hope*

More Faith in My Day

More Hours in My Day

*Quiet Moments for
a Busy Mom's Soul*

A Quiet Refuge

Safe in the Father's Hands

*Simple Secrets to
a Beautiful Home*

*Strength for Today,
Bright Hope for Tomorrow*

The Twelve Teas® of Inspiration

A Tea to Comfort Your Soul

*The Twelve Teas®
of Celebration*

*The Twelve Teas®
of Friendship*

More Great Books from — Harvest House Publishers

MEN ARE LIKE WAFFLES—WOMEN ARE LIKE SPAGHETTI
Bill and Pam Farrel

Bill and Pam explain why a man is like a waffle (each element of his life is in a separate box), why a woman is like spaghetti (everything in her life touches everything else), and what these differences mean. Then they show you how to achieve more satisfying relationships. Biblical insights, sound research, humorous anecdotes, and real-life stories make this guide entertaining and practical. Much of the material in this rewarding book will also improve interactions with family, friends, and coworkers.

THE RELATIONSHIP DOCTOR'S PRESCRIPTION FOR BETTER COMMUNICATION IN YOUR MARRIAGE
Dr. David Hawkins

Couples thrive when they honestly share their perspectives and feelings, learn to disagree, and trust one another to support and strengthen each other and not injure or ridicule. This user-friendly manual helps you recognize ineffective patterns of relating in your marriage and offers constructive alternatives. You'll find practical steps you can take to replace defensiveness with openness and compassion, develop more transparency, and achieve greater trust and emotional intimacy. Transform your marriage by developing your communication skills!

FEARLESS FAITH
Living Beyond the Walls of Safe Christianity
John Fischer

It's not always easy to be a Christian these days. We live in a culture that frequently challenges the very foundations of our faith. Our natural response is to flee from the criticisms and the negative influences that surround us, creating our own safe Christian environment in an unsafe world. But that's not what Jesus intended. In this provocative book, Fischer reminds us that we are to be in the world—part of the dialogue—and making a contribution to every area of our lives from a perspective of faith.

A MAN AFTER GOD'S OWN HEART
Jim George

Do you want to be a man after God's own heart? Jim shows that a heartfelt desire to grow spiritually is all that's needed. God's grace does the rest, bringing lasting change to a man's marriage, work, and witness. Realize the tremendous joy and confidence that comes from pursuing God in every area of your life.

CONVERSATION WITH GOD
Lloyd John Ogilvie

Bestselling author Lloyd Ogilvie delivers a fresh approach to prayer—one that is as much listening as speaking. Drawing on years of experiencing God as a friend, Ogilvie clearly and simply explains the many dimensions of prayer and then provides a 30-day prayer guide. As you begin to enjoy give-and-take conversation with God as a part of everyday life, you'll experience the truth that He is always available, that you are never alone or isolated. Prayer will become more refreshing, profound, and meaningful than you ever have thought possible! Excellent for Bible studies or individual study.

KNOWING GOD 101
Bruce Bickel and Stan Jantz

This book is brimming with joy! You'll love the inspiring descriptions of God's nature, His personality, and His activities. Curious inquirers and earnest seekers will find straightforward responses to essential questions about God, including: Eternity, where did God come from? The trinity, is God three people or one? The Bible, did God really communicate His own thoughts to us?

WHAT EVERY PARENT NEEDS TO KNOW ABOUT VIDEO GAMES
Richard Abanes

Packed with the latest information on the pros and cons of video and computer gaming, this concise, easy-to-follow guide helps you understand a form of entertainment that's part of the daily lives of your kids. Bestselling author Richard Abanes—an experienced video-gamer himself—offers balanced discussions of positives and negatives of game-playing, family-friendly selections...and those that aren't, terminology and genres explanations, and ways to evaluate a game's overall message.

HARRY POTTER, NARNIA, AND THE LORD OF THE RINGS
What You Need to Know About Fantasy Books and Movies

Richard Abanes

Is every fantasy story appropriate for everyone? In this evenhanded exploration of the books of J.K. Rowling, C.S. Lewis, and J.R.R. Tolkien, as well as the films based on their writings, Richard Abanes—a fantasy fan himself—answers key questions that include: 1) What is inspiring and healthy in these works? What is misleading and harmful? 2) Do I need to be concerned about occult influence from fantasy? 3) How do movies and merchandising impact kids' minds?

HOW TO TALK TO YOUR KIDS ABOUT DRUGS
Stephen Arterburn and Jim Burns

Kids can't avoid being exposed to drug use today, some even as early as grade school. What can you do to protect them? Packed with practical information and time-proven prevention techniques, *How to Talk to Your Kids About Drugs* is a realistic, up-to-date, comprehensive plan for drug-proofing your kids. And if your children are already using alcohol or drugs, respected counselor Stephen Arterburn and well-known parenting and family expert Jim Burns offer step-by-step advice to get them straight and sober. Get the knowledge and tools you need to help your kids stay or become drug free. Includes helpful study guide.

HARVEST HOUSE
PUBLISHERS